Survey of
Instructional Development Models

Third Edition

by

Kent L. Gustafson

Robert Maribe Branch

May, 1997

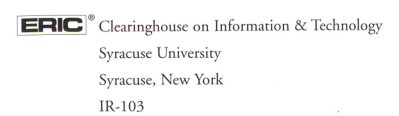 Clearinghouse on Information & Technology

Syracuse University

Syracuse, New York

IR-103

Survey of Instructional Development Models

Third Edition

by Kent L. Gustafson and Robert Maribe Branch

This publication is available from Information Resources Publications, Syracuse University, 4-194 Center for Science and Technology, Syracuse, New York 13244-4100; 1-800-464-9107 (IR-103)

ISBN: 0-937597-43-0

This publication is prepared with funding from the Office of Educational Research and Improvement, U.S. Department of Education, under contract no. RR93002009. The opinions expressed in this report do not necessarily reflect the positions or policies of OERI or ED.

Eric Plotnick, Editor in Chief

Susann L. Wurster, Copy Editor and Designer

About the Authors

Kent Gustafson is a professor in the Department of Instructional Technology at the University of Georgia in Athens, Georgia. He has served as professor at Michigan State University, director of media services for a regional school district, and classroom teacher of mathematics. He holds degrees from Worcester State College, the University of Massachusetts, and Michigan State University. His current areas of interest include managing the instructional design process, analyzing performance problems, and designing computer-based tools to support instructional development. Dr. Gustafson has authored numerous publications including three books: *Instructional Technology* with Fred Knirk, the second edition of *Instructional Design* with Murray Tillman and the late Leslie Briggs, and *Research for School Media Specialists* with Jane Smith. He is an active member of several professional associations including AECT and AERA. He is a member of the Editorial Board of the Development section of Educational Technology Research and Development.

Kent L. Gustafson

Rob Branch is an associate professor in the Department of Instructional Technology at the University of Georgia in Athens, Georgia. Prior to coming to the University of Georgia, he served as associate professor of Instructional Design, Development and Evaluation at Syracuse University, where he was also associate director of the ERIC Clearinghouse on Information & Technology. Dr. Branch has also worked as a classroom teacher of technological studies. He holds degrees from Elizabeth City State University, Ball State University, and Virginia Tech University. His primary area of interest lies in the accurate portrayal of the instructional design and development process. Dr. Branch has authored numerous journal articles, and currently serves as senior editor for the *Educational Media and Technology Yearbook*. He is an active member of several professional associations including AECT, ISPI and AERA.

Robert Maribe Branch

Table of Contents

List of Figures

Foreword

In the third edition of *Survey of Instructional Development Models*, Gustafson and Branch present the reader with an update to this popular ERIC/IT monograph. It is worthy to note that while previous editions were published approximately ten years apart, this edition comes just six years after its predecessor publication. This is an indication of the increasing numbers of ID models being presented and discussed in the literature. I hope that this is also an indication of the growing use of ID models in education and training at all levels.

This monograph is not meant to be an exhaustive reporting on all ID models, past and present. Rather this monograph provides an overview, trends, and analysis of ID models in general, and selected models in particular. The authors carefully explain the selection criteria used to determine which ID models would be presented in detail in this monograph. ID models have been classified into one of three groups: classroom orientation; product orientation; and system orientation. Although necessarily broad, the three groups adequately distinguish among the levels of instructional development processes found in common practice today.

Where does this monograph fit into the schema of publications focused on the application of the ID process currently available today? Clearly, *Survey of Instructional Development Models* should be required reading for every student seeking a degree in Instructional Systems Technology.

It is an excellent first introduction to the ID process and provides a solid foundation for future study. It will also serve as a valuable reference document for instructional technologists working to introduce the ID process into public and private schools, into higher education institutions, and into a new corporate training environment. It probably should be required reading for every school principal and superintendent as well as every corporate manager responsible for training programs. This monograph is an excellent tool for the novice and the veteran involved with the ID process.

Education and training are changing more rapidly today than ever before. In places where these changes have been significant and successful, the application of instructional development models and processes has been a key factor. This monograph adds to the body of literature that will help continue and enhance the process of educational change as we move into the next century.

Stanley D. Zenor

Executive Director

Association for Educational Communications and Technology (AECT)

Survey of

Instructional Development Models

Third Edition

Introduction

Purpose

In this ERIC monograph, we update and expand upon earlier ERIC publications by Twelker et al. (1972) and Gustafson (1981, 1991) on the topic of instructional development (ID) models. Since ID models first appeared in the literature in the 1960s, an increasing number of models have been published in the instructional technology and other education literature. This monograph presents a very brief history of ID models, describes a taxonomy for classifying them, provides examples from each of the categories in the taxonomy, and describes trends in their content and focus.

Only a few ID models are described in detail in this survey. Selection was difficult because there are literally hundreds of ID models in the literature. Selection criteria included: the historical significance of the model, its unique structure or perspective, and its general distribution. It was also necessary to select models that matched each of the categories in the classification taxonomy. As a result, many excellent models are not included in this survey. Models that represent only part of the ID process (e.g. only needs assessment, media selection, lesson design, or evaluation) were not selected. The ID models that were selected are representative of the ID literature, and among them, contain most of the main concepts found in other models.

Definition of Instructional Development

One of the major problems plaguing the field of educational technology is inconsistent use of technical terminology. The term instructional development is no exception. Although several attempts have been made to define the field and derive a standard set of meanings for various terms (Ely, 1973; AECT, 1977; Ely, 1983; Seels & Richey, 1994), the results have not been widely adopted and used in the literature. For our purposes, we could use either the currently circulating definition created by Seels and Richey or the Association for Educational Communications and Technology (AECT) definition used in earlier editions of this monograph. Seels and Richey use the term "instructional systems design" (ISD) instead of instructional development, and define it as "an organized procedure that includes the steps of analyzing, designing, developing, implementing, and evaluating instruction" (p 31). Their definition is similar to the way an AECT (1977) committee chaired by Kenneth Silber defined instructional development almost two decades earlier:

> A systematic approach to the design, production, evaluation, and utilization of complete systems of instruction, including all appropriate components and a management pattern for using them; instructional development is larg-

10

er than instructional product development, which is concerned with only isolated products, and is larger than
instructional design, which is only one phase of instructional development. (p. 172)

Both definitions encompass a wide array of activities ranging from an initial sensing of a concern that "something" ought to be done, to implementing and evaluating the instruction that is developed. Consistent to
both definitions is the notion that instructional development is far more
inclusive than activities associated with preparing lesson specifications,
determining moment-to-moment instructional strategies, sequencing,
providing motivational elements, and determining learner actions. These
activities are often labeled instructional design, but also have been called
instructional development by some authors.

Another term that has been used inconsistently is "system." The term system is used in at least three different ways. Some authors use the term system to describe the outcomes or products of the instructional development effort. From this perspective, the learner environment and its related management and support components together comprise an instructional system. Another, but less common, use of the term system, is in the
context of general systems theory (GST). Within this perspective, numerous general system theory concepts (e.g., open and closed systems,
entropy, and interdependence), are applied when describing the instructional development process. The third perspective is equivalent with how
we have chosen to define instructional development below.

In some respects, professionals find themselves in an Alice in Wonderland
setting where any term means whatever the author wants it to mean. For
this reason, we have found it desirable to create a taxonomy for classifying
models. By carefully examining each model, we can determine what activities its creator is describing. We can also determine the goals and the settings in which the activities are to occur. We are then in a better position
to understand what the authors are describing even when the terminology is inconsistent from model to model.

11

In summary, several different and inconsistent uses of terminology are frequently employed by authors when describing the comprehensive process we call instructional development. In our definition, instructional development consists of at least four major activities:

- Analysis of the setting and learner needs;

- Design of a set of specifications for an effective, efficient, and relevant learner environment;

- Development of all learner and management materials; and

- Evaluation of the results of the development both formatively and summatively.

A fifth activity may be added, involving distribution and monitoring of the learning environment across varied settings, perhaps over an extended period of time.

Assumptions

Because we place great emphasis on identifying the assumptions made by the creators of the ID models we review in this monograph, it seems appropriate that we explain our own assumptions about the ID process, and about ID model building and application. First and foremost, we are attempting to encourage better understanding and utilization of ID models. A greater awareness of instructional development, and the models used to portray the process, will be of benefit to both long-time practitioners and those new to the field. Secondly, we believe there is enough room within the fundamental concept of the instructional development process to incorporate most of the emerging theories and philosophies of learning, and to incorporate advances in the technology available for design, development, and delivery of instruction. Thirdly, our definition of the process, our vision of the role of models, and our taxonomy for classifying them, are based on the following explicit assumptions:

1. Instructional development models serve as conceptual and communi-
    cation tools for analyzing, designing, creating, and evaluating guided
    learning ranging from broad educational environments to narrow
    training applications.

2. The greater the compatibility between a model of instructional devel-
    opment and its contextual, theoretical, philosophical, and phenome-
    nological origins, the greater the potential for success in constructing
    effective episodes of guided learning.

3. Instructional development modeling is one way to take into account:
    the multiple backgrounds of learners; the multiple interactions that
    may occur during learning; the variety of contexts in which learning
    is situated; and the necessity to guide, manage, and communicate the
    ID process.

4. There is a requirement to focus on conceptualizations of instruction-
    al development models that are broader than the conceptualizations
    often associated with industrialized, militaristic and positivistic preci-
    sion.

5. A taxonomy of ID models should be based on categories of contextu-
    al factors, learner expectations, and type of desired knowledge or skill.

6. There will continue to be an interest in ID models. However, the level
    of specificity at which they are applied will change.

Early ID Models

Of necessity, we must pick an arbitrary date from which to begin to trace
the origins of the ID model building process. Otherwise we could make
the case that the creators of the earliest recorded cave drawings, and the
scribes who produced papyrus scrolls, represent the pioneers of systemat-

ic instruction. Similarly, many of the ideas and procedures commonly found in ID models (e.g. job analysis, measurable objectives, and performance testing) predate the period generally accepted as representing the beginnings of ID model building.

The specific term "instructional development," defined as a systematic process for improving instruction, appears to have its origins in a project conducted at Michigan State University from 1961-1965. Entitled "Instructional Systems Development: A Demonstration and Evaluation Project" (Barson, 1967), this project, directed by Dr. John Barson, produced one of the earliest ID models. The setting for Barson's model and related project was higher education, and the goal was improvement of college courses. Barson's model was reviewed in the first ERIC monograph in this series by Twelker et al. The reader is also referred to the Barson project final report (ED 020 673) for more details. The Barson model is notable in that it is one of the few ID models ever subjected to evaluation in a variety of projects at a variety of institutions. The Barson project also produced a set of heuristics (e.g., take the faculty members out of their own discipline when showing them examples) for instructional developers. These heuristics provided the basis for much of the early research on the ID process, and also served as a general guide for instructional developers in higher education.

Early work by a number of other authors also produced ID models, although the specific term "instructional development" was not used. For example, the developers of programmed instruction (c.f., Markle, 1964, 1978) often applied a systematic process, but they generally did not recognize the major contribution of the tryout and revision process to the successes they recorded. In the 1950s and 1960s, one of the most influential ID model builders was L. C. Silvern (1965). Silvern's work with the military and aerospace industry resulted in an extremely complex and detailed model (with multiple variations) that drew heavily on general systems theory. That model is not widely circulated today, but remains an excellent source document for those willing to wade through Silvern's sometimes obscure writing. Students of the ID process will readily see Silvern's influence on the content of contemporary models.

The ID model developed by Hamreus (1968), while he taught at the Teaching Research Division of the Oregon State System of Higher Education, is another classic. One of Hamreus' significant contributions was his presentation of both "maxi" and "mini" versions of the model. This "two-size" approach was based on Hamreus' belief that there is a requirement for a simple model to communicate with clients, and a necessity for a more detailed operational version for those developers working on the project. Hamreus' model provided the basic structure for the Instructional Development Institute (IDI) model (National Special Media Institutes, 1971). The IDI model received extremely wide distribution, and was among the best known ID models in the United States in the 1970s and 1980s. National Special Media Institutes created a five-day workshop for teachers and administrators, and by the late 1970s, the workshops had been offered to over 20,000 public school personnel. The materials from IDI workshops were also extensively used by graduate programs of that era to introduce students to the basic concepts of the ID process. Seels and Glasgow (1990) reproduced and described the IDI model in their book on the ID process. Since Hamreus' model was extensively reviewed in the Twelker monograph, the reader is referred there for details. Because of the IDI model's wide circulation and influence on the field, we will discuss it again later in this monograph.

Other Reviews of ID Models

In addition to the Twelker (1972) review, at least four other major reviews of ID models worthy of study have been conducted. In 1972, Stamas reviewed 23 models to determine whether or not each included a list of components he felt were part of the ID process. That study, originally part of a doctoral dissertation at Michigan State University (Stamas, 1973), was reproduced as an occasional paper by the Division of Instructional Development of the Association for Educational Communications and Technology. In 1980, Andrews and Goodson reviewed 40 models in the *Journal of Instructional Development* (Andrews & Goodson, 1980). Like Stamas, they developed a matrix of ID elements, and analyzed the models for their inclusion of those elements. Andrews and Goodson also attempted to trace a logical progression or evolution of later models from earlier ones, but were unable to detect any pattern. Their findings add weight to the view that the literature on ID models is circular rather than cumulative, with little unique substance being added as the years progress.

More recently, Salisbury (1990) reviewed a number of ID models found in major textbooks in the field to assess the degree to which they contained specific references to a range of general systems theory concepts. He concluded that most models contained few specific references to those general systems concepts contained in his matrix. Edmonds, Branch and Mukherjee (1994) presented the results of an extensive review of ID models as a way to address the proliferation of instructional development variation applications during the past decade. They concluded that an ID model is understood better when it is classified by its context and by the level of application for which it is intended.

Taken together, these reviews provide an excellent sampling of the array of existing ID models, and suggest alternate perspectives on how the models might be examined. The conclusion we can draw from all of these reviews is that the overall ID process, as originally conceived, has not changed significantly even though additional theories, additional tools for design, development, and delivery, and additional procedures are now being used by those engaged in instructional development.

16

Chapter

1

The Role of Models in

Instructional Development

Why should we have models? Models help us conceptualize representations of reality. A model is a simple representation of more complex forms, processes, and functions of physical phenomena or ideas.

The physical and natural sciences use models for theory building and for testing, describing, predicting, and explaining. The role of models in instructional development is to: provide us with conceptual and communication tools that we can use to visualize, direct, and manage processes for generating episodes of guided learning; allow us to view both the linear and concurrent aspects of instructional development; and to allow us to select or develop appropriate operational tools.

Conceptual and Communication Tools

Instructional development is a complex, yet purposeful, process that promotes creativity, interactivity and cyberneticity. Instructional development models convey the guiding principles for analyzing, producing and revising episodes of guided learning. Both established and newer ID models accommodate emerging theories about planned learning, and the broad array of contexts in which ID models are being applied. Philosophical orientation and theoretical perspective frame the concepts upon which ID models are constructed. The more compatible the theory and philosophy are to the context in which a model is to be applied, the greater the potential that the original purpose of the ID model will be achieved.

Instructional development models communicate their associated processes visually by illustrating the procedures that make it possible to produce instruction. Instructional development models should provide communication tools for: determining appropriate outcomes; collecting data; analyzing data; generating learning strategies; selecting or constructing media; authentic assessment; revision; and implementation. Figure 1 shows a conceptual relationship among the core elements of the ID process.

While a conceptual display of the core elements of the ID process is helpful, we also must indicate *how to practice* particular elements of the ID process. Conceptual tools for analyzing, categorizing, and measuring learning outcomes identify the types of contexts in which an ID model

18

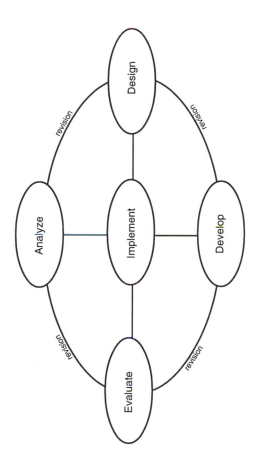

Figure 1. Core elements of instructional development.

may be utilized. Directions for generating and utilizing appropriate strategies, procedures, job aids, and other conceptual tools are also significant
criteria for selecting an ID model. Once the conceptual tools are matched
to the context in which the ID model is to be applied, the model guides
the developer in the selection or development of the operational tools that
are necessary for completion of the instructional development process.
Specific procedures for conceptualizing, planning, conducting, and managing the ID process can be implemented with operational tools that may
or may not be identified as part of the ID model.

Linear and Concurrent Aspects of ID

The instructional development process can be approached as a single linear process, or as a set of concurrent procedures. Instructional development should be portrayed in ways that communicate the true richness and
reality associated with planning interactive instruction. Many ID models
are interpreted as stifling, passive, lock-step, and simple, because of the
visual elements used to compose the model (Branch, 1997). Instructional
development models have traditionally been portrayed as rectilinear rows
of boxes connected by straight lines with one-way arrows and a return line
that is parallel to other straight lines (Figure 2). Rectilinear portrayals of
ID models often do not acknowledge the specific complexities associated
with the instructional development process. Curvilinear compositions of
ovals connected by curved lines with two-way arrows can better acknowledge the complex reality upon which the ID process is modeled (Figure
3). However, there remains an implied sequence, at least among the core
elements.

In another approach, the ID process can be modeled as sets of concurrent
procedures. Portraying ID as sets of procedures occurring simultaneously,
or as overlapping procedures during the process, tends to communicate
more of the simultaneous iterations that characterize the way instructional development is commonly practiced (Rowland, 1992). The selection of
an appropriate model for an instructional development context may

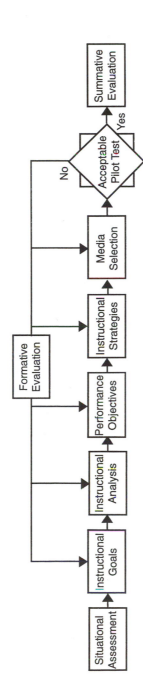

Figure 2. **Rectilinear** portrayal of instructional development process.

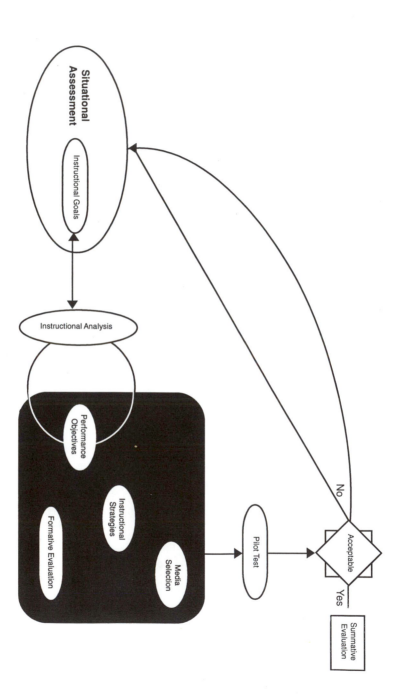

Figure 3. Curvilinear portrayal of instructional development process.

depend on the desire or requirement to reflect the degree of linearity that is likely to be followed during the process. Tripp and Bichelmeyer's (1990) Rapid Prototyping model (Figure 4) is an example of how the core elements of instructional development can overlap in a highly interactive series of design and test cycles, especially when the goals are formative, and immediate products are required. Wedman and Tessmer's (1991) Layers of Necessity model (Figure 5) is an example of the portrayal of an overall ID process wherein each layer is a self-contained ID model that is adjusted for time, resources and project scope.

Operational Tools

An ID model should contain enough detail to establish guidelines for managing the people, places, and things that will interact together, and to estimate the resources required to complete a project. Instructional development models can directly or indirectly specify products, such as time lines, samples of work, deliverables, and periodic endorsements by appropriate supervisory personnel.

While models provide the conceptual reference, they also provide the framework for selecting or constructing the operational tools required to apply the model. Operational tools such as PERT charts, nominal group techniques, task analysis diagrams, lesson plan templates, worksheets for generating objectives, and production schedule templates contextualize the ID process. Some ID models include highly prescriptive information about how to develop the companion tools; or provide most of the tools necessary to apply the process. Other ID models provide only a conceptual diagram, without any operational tools or directions for constructing the companion tools necessary for applying a particular ID process. The Interservices Procedures for Instructional Systems Development model (Branson, 1975) is an example of a highly prescriptive ID model that has a comprehensive set of companion operational tools. The Dick and Carey (1996) model is an example of a moderately prescriptive ID model that has a sufficient set of companion operational tools. Several ID models

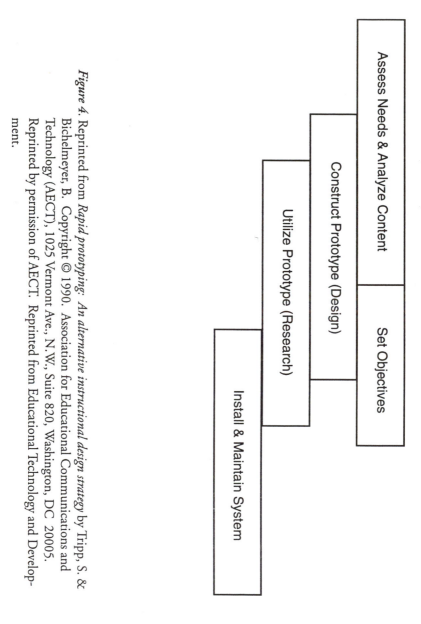

Figure 4. Reprinted from *Rapid prototyping: An alternative instructional design strategy* by Tripp, S. & Bichelmeyer, B. Copyright © 1990. Association for Educational Communications and Technology (AECT), 1025 Vermont Ave., N.W., Suite 820, Washington, DC 20005. Reprinted by permission of AECT. Reprinted from Educational Technology and Development.

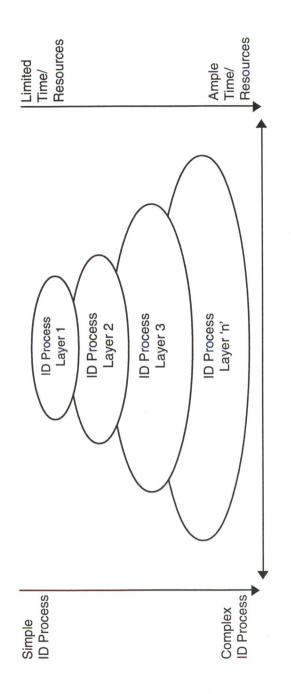

Figure 5. Reprinted from *Adapting instructional design to project circumstance: The layers of necessity model* by Wedman, J. & Tessmer, M. Copyright © 1991. Reprinted by permission of Educational Technology Publications.

merely diagram and do not specify any accompanying operational tools, or provide directions for constructing the tools required to apply the process. Tools used to apply the ID process (Zemke & Kramlinger, 1984) can be used with different models when appropriate. Operational tools have even been developed separately from a companion ID model, such as in the case of Greer (1992), who developed generic tools and techniques that can be used for managing an ID project. Thus, another selection criterion for selecting an appropriate ID model is whether or not the author has included companion operational tools and procedures for applying the model, (or included directions for their construction), and specified the degree to which they can be applied (directly or in modified form) in the current context.

Models of instructional development vary widely in their purposes, amount of detail provided, degree of linearity in which they are applied, and quantity, quality, and relevance of the accompanying operational tools. While no single model is useful for all settings and all purposes, it is important that we identify the intended focus of an ID model and the context for which it was intended. The following taxonomy of ID models can help guide the way in which we adopt or adapt instructional development models.

Chapter

2

A Taxonomy of ID Models

Instructional development is being practiced in a variety of settings and various models have been created reflecting those variations. A taxonomy of ID models can help clarify the underlying assumptions of each model, and help identify the conditions under which each might be most appropriately applied.

Although the number of ID models published far exceeds the number of unique environments in which they are applied, there are several substantive differences among models. Thus, there is some value in creating a taxonomy for classifying them. A taxonomy can also help organize the extensive literature on this topic, and perhaps also assist instructional developers in selecting a model that is best matched to a given set of circumstances.

One such taxonomy has been created by Gustafson (1981, 1991). Gustafson's schema contains three categories into which models can be placed. Placement of any model in one of the categories is based on the set of assumptions that its creator has made, often implicitly, about the conditions under which both the development and delivery of instruction will occur. For example, the models by Gerlach and Ely (1980) and by Heinich, Molenda, Russell, and Smaldino (1996) are clearly intended for use by classroom teachers, probably working alone as both designers and deliverers of instruction. Conversely, Bergman and Moore (1990) describe how their model can be used by a team that includes instructional developers, production staff, computer programmers, and a project manager to develop multimedia-based instructional products. Their model implicitly assumes that no members of the development team will actually have a role in the product's ultimate implementation or use.

The models by Dick and Carey (1996), Smith and Ragan (1993), and Gagné, Briggs and Wager (1992) represent still a third category of ID models that appear to be intended for use in a variety of organizational settings. It seems most likely that each of these models will be used by a skilled development team to develop a complex "system" of instruction to meet specified organizational requirements or goals. The Branson model (1975) for military training and the National Special Media Institute model (1971) for education also assume there will be a large-scale, team-oriented development effort.

The taxonomy presented in Figure 6 can be used to categorize ID models based on a number of assumptions their creators have made about the settings in which the models would be applied, and how the process might

28

take place. This taxonomy includes three categories indicating whether the model is best applied for developing: individual classroom instruction; products for implementation by users other than the developers; or large and complex instructional systems directed at an organization's problems or goals.

A matrix relating the three classes of models (classroom, product, and system) to the nine characteristics mentioned below is presented in Figure 6. The comments in each cell of the matrix indicate how each characteristic is typically viewed by those having that perspective. Examples of how the characteristics relate to each class of model are described below.

The assumptions examined to decide how a model should be categorized are:

- typical output in terms of amount of instruction prepared

- resources committed to the development effort

- whether it is a team or individual effort

- ID skill and experience of the individual or team

- whether most instructional materials will be selected from existing sources or represent original design and production

- amount of preliminary (front-end) analysis conducted

- anticipated technological complexity of the learning environment

- amount of tryout and revision conducted, and

- amount of dissemination and follow-up occurring after development.

Selected Characteristics	Classroom Orientation	Product Orientation	System Orientation
Typical Output	One or a Few Hours of Instruction	Self Instructional or Instructor-Delivered Package	Course or Entire Curriculum
Resources Committed to Development	Very Low	High	High
Team or Individual Effort	Individual	Usually a Team	Team
ID Skill/Experience	Low	High	High/Very High
Emphasis on Development or Selection	Select	Develop	Develop
Amount of Front-End Analysis/Needs Assessment	Low	Low to Medium	Very High
Technological Complexity of Delivery Media	Low	Medium to High	Medium to High
Amount of Tryout and Revision	Low to Medium	Very High	Medium to High
Amount of Distribution/Dissemination	None	High	Medium to High

Figure 6. A taxonomy of instructional development models based on selected characteristics.

30

As we noted earlier, most authors of ID models do not explicitly discuss any of the assumptions listed above. Rather, they simply describe their model's major elements and how they are to be implemented. The assumptions we use for classifying each model we discuss in Figure 6 were derived solely by us based upon our review of the descriptive material accompanying the model.

Heinich, Molenda, Russell, and Smaldino (1996) and Reiser and Dick (1996) offer a **classroom perspective** on how to practice instructional development. Each set of authors makes the assumptions that: the size of the planned instructional event will be small; the amount of resources available will be low; it will be an individual rather than a team effort; the teacher is not a trained instructional developer (although it is hoped that the teacher will have gained some of those skills by studying the text), and that the teacher will generally be limited to selecting and adapting existing materials rather than creating new ones. Additionally, the classroom perspective typically assumes that: little time will be devoted to front-end analysis; the learning environment will likely be relatively "low-tech"; the amount of tryout and revision will be limited; and the amount of dissemination beyond that classroom will be very low. This is not to say that classroom teachers never work on large scale development efforts that involve a team, extensive resources, a high-tech environment, and extensive analysis, tryout, revision, and dissemination of what was developed. However, if teachers were to be involved in such a project, the Heinich, Molenda, Russell and Smaldino model would no longer be their best choice since the assumptions would be entirely different.

Product development models such as Bergman and Moore (1990) make different assumptions, including one that assumes that there will be a specific product created of a few hours or days in length. Product development models also assume that substantial resources are available to a team of highly trained individuals including a professional manager. Typically the team will produce original materials, perhaps to be commercially marketed. The amount of front-end analysis varies widely, and a technically sophisticated product often results. Tryout and revision are usually extensive, and wide dissemination of the product is common.

31

System oriented models, such as Branson (1975), Dick and Carey (1996), and Smith and Ragan (1993) typically assume that a substantial amount of instruction such as an entire course or entire curriculum will be created. Substantial resources are typically provided to a team of skilled instructional developers and subject matter experts. Whether or not original production or selection of materials will occur varies, but in some cases original development may be required. Assumptions about the technological sophistication of the delivery system also vary, and the decision on a delivery system is often based on the infrastructure available for course delivery. The amount of front-end analysis is usually high, as is the amount of tryout and revision. Dissemination and utilization may be quite wide, but probably does not involve the team that did the development.

In summary, our taxonomy places ID models in one of three categories based on the assumptions made by the models' creators. Of course, many ID models can be, and no doubt are, used successfully under different sets of assumptions. Nonetheless, classifying models does have the advantage of exposing their assumptions to analysis, and perhaps assisting users in selecting models that are most appropriate for particular situations.

Chapter

3

Classroom Orientation

Assumptions

Classroom **ID models** are of interest primarily to professional teachers who accept as a given that their role is to teach, and that their students require some form of instruction. Users of classroom ID models include elementary and secondary school teachers, community college and vocational school instructors, and university faculty. Some training programs in business and industry also assume a classroom orientation.

As we have indicated, there is a wide variety of classroom settings. Most teachers assume (with real justification) that students will be assigned to or will enroll voluntarily in their classes, and that there will be a specified number of class meetings, each of a pre-determined length. The teacher's role is to decide on appropriate content, plan instructional strategies, identify appropriate media, deliver the instruction, and evaluate learners. Due to the on-going nature of classroom instruction, often accompanied by a heavy teaching load, the typical classroom teacher has little time for comprehensive development of instructional materials. Resources for development are also usually limited. Therefore, the teacher needs to identify existing resources that can be adapted to existing conditions, rather than engage in original development. Furthermore, many elementary and secondary teachers teach a given instructional topic only once a year, so they might have less concern for the rigorous formative evaluation associated with courses and workshops that are offered on a repetitive basis.

Teaching personnel usually view an ID model as a general road map to follow. Typically, a classroom ID model outlines only a few functions, and simply provides a guide for the teacher. It should be noted that although there are a number of classroom oriented ID models, they are not widely known by teachers or adopted by them. The developer, who works with teachers within the given conditions and assumptions described above, would do well to employ any ID model with caution, because teachers are not likely to be familiar with the concepts or processes of systematic instructional development. Teachers may also view the process depicted by many ID models as being mechanistic and likely to result in dehumanized instruction.

However, the models discussed below have been found to be acceptable and readily understandable by at least some teachers, and represent a class of models with which all developers should be familiar. Four models have been selected to represent the variety of ID models most applicable in the classroom environment: Gerlach and Ely (1980); Kemp, Morrison and Ross (1994); Heinich, Molenda, Russell and Smaldino (1996); and Reiser and Dick (1996).

The Gerlach and Ely Model

The entry point of the Gerlach and Ely (1980) model (Figure 7) calls for the identification of content and the specification of objectives as simultaneous, interactive activities. While Gerlach and Ely clearly prefer the approach of specifying objectives as a "first task," they recognize that many teachers think about instruction from the standpoint of content first. Their model is one of only a few that recognize the content orientation of many teachers. In this model, learning objectives are to be written and classified before several design decisions are to be made. Their classification scheme is based on Gerlach's other scholarly work, and presents a five-part cognitive taxonomy with single categories for affective and motor skill objectives.

The next step in their model is the assessment of the entry behavior of learners, a step common to many classroom oriented models. However, despite the specification of entry behavior as a major step in the ID process, few concrete procedures for doing so are provided in this model. The next step is really five activities to be performed simultaneously. These activities are viewed as interactive, with any decision in one area influencing the range of decisions available in the others: e.g., the design process is itself a system. The five activities are: (1) determine strategy, (2) organize groups, (3) allocate time, (4) allocate space, and (5) select resources.

Under strategies, they posit a continuum from exposition (all cues) to discovery (no cues). The teacher/designer's role is to select one or more strategies along this continuum. Students can be organized into configurations ranging from self-study to whole-class activities based on strategies, space, time, and resources. Time is viewed as a constant to be divided up among various strategies. Space is not a constant because teachers can and should extend learning experiences beyond the classroom, and the classroom itself can usually be rearranged for different grouping patterns.

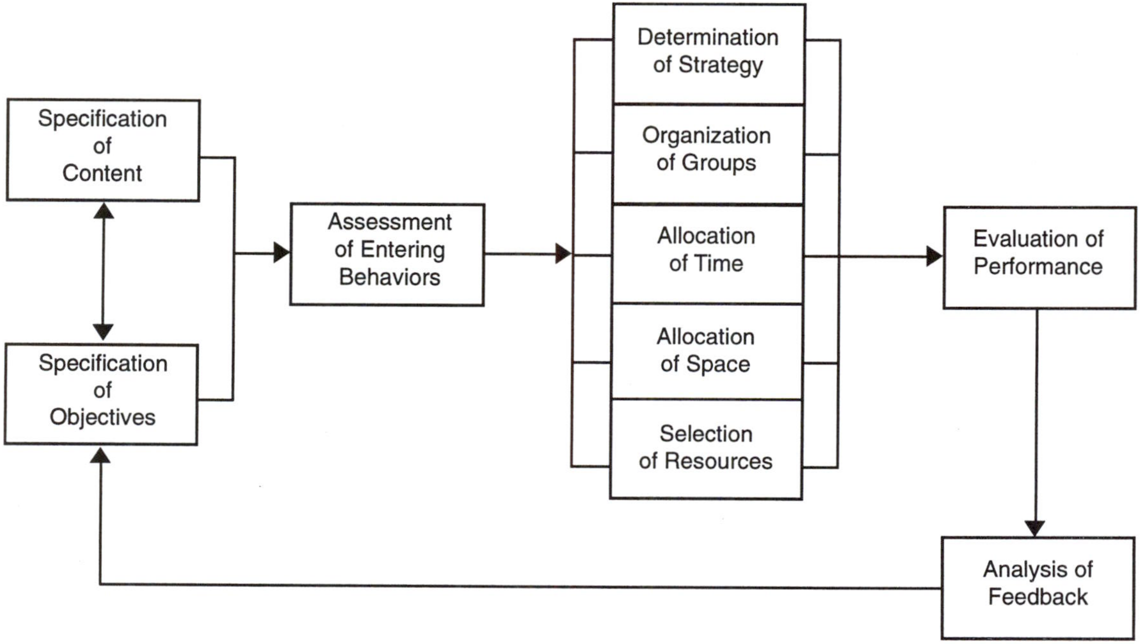

Figure 7. Reprinted from *Teaching and media: A systematic approach* (2nd ed.), by Gerlach, V. S., & Ely, D. P. Copyright © 1980. All rights reserved. Reprinted/adapted by permission of Allyn & Bacon.

Selection of resources focuses on the teacher's need to locate, obtain, and adapt or supplement existing instructional materials. Emphasis is placed on where and how to find such resources, and also on the importance of previewing and planning for the use of these resources as part of the overall instructional strategy. The emphasis on selecting rather then developing instructional materials is a common feature of classroom oriented ID models.

Evaluation of student performance follows the five simultaneous decisions described above. Evaluation directs the teacher/designer's attention to measuring student achievement and student attitude toward the content and instruction. Evaluation is seen as closely linked to the learner objectives stated earlier, and attention is also directed to evaluating the "system" itself. The last step in the Gerlach and Ely model is provision of feedback to the teacher regarding the effectiveness of the instruction. Feedback focuses on reviewing all earlier steps in the model, with special emphasis placed on re-examining decisions regarding the objectives and strategies selected.

The Gerlach and Ely model is a mix of linear and concurrent development activities. Several steps are seen as simultaneous, but the model is generally linear in its orientation. Its main strength is that practicing classroom teachers can readily identify with the process it describes. Its objectives-classification taxonomy is simple and non-threatening to teachers. The authors also relate their taxonomy to specific instructional strategies. This model's main weakness is that it may unintentionally reinforce teachers and administrators in maintaining existing organization and staffing patterns rather than in encouraging them to re-examine the entire basis of how schools should operate.

The Kemp, Morrison and Ross Model

Kemp, Morrison and Ross (1994) present an instructional development model (Figure 8) with a focus on curriculum planning. Kemp's (1985)

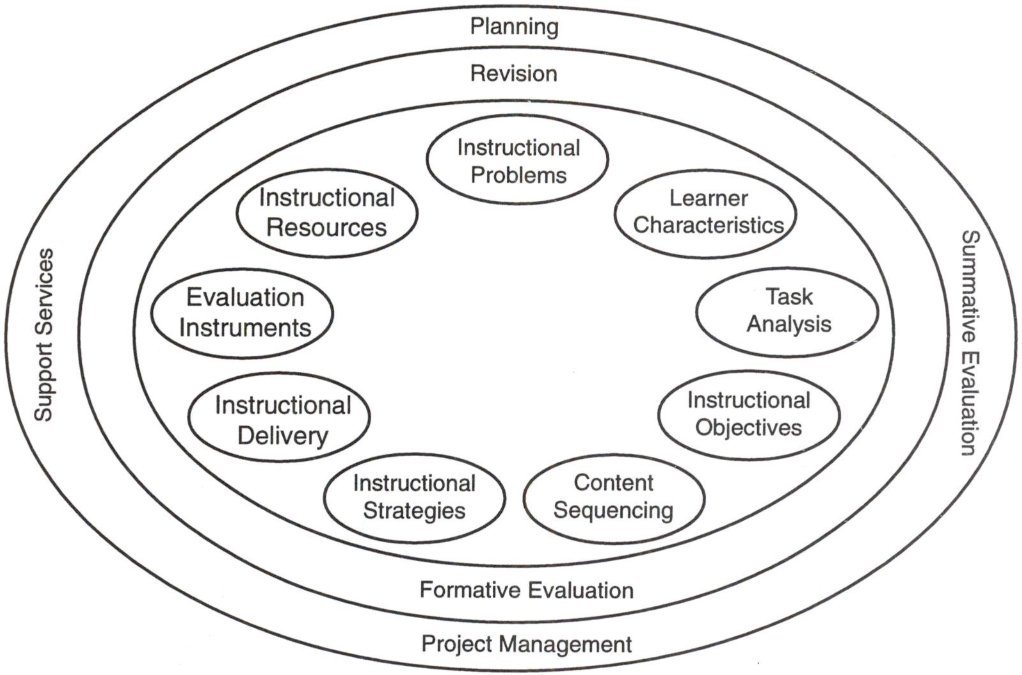

Figure 8. Reprinted from *Designing effective instruction* by Kemp, J. E., Morrison, G. R., & Ross, S. Copyright © 1994. Reprinted by permission of Prentice-Hall, Inc., Upper Saddle River, NJ.

earlier ID model is modified to include project management and support services as components of the process. Kemp, Morrison and Ross approach "instruction from the perspective of the learner rather than from the perspective of the content, the traditional approach" (p. 6). They focus on answering the following questions:

- What level of readiness do individual students have for accomplishing the objectives?

- What teaching and learning methods are most appropriate in terms of objectives and student characteristics?

- What media or other resources are most suitable?

- What support, beyond the teacher and the available resources, is needed for successful learning?

- How is achievement of objectives determined?

- What revisions are necessary if a tryout of the program does not match expectations? (p. 6)

Based on the identified key factors, Kemp, Morrison and Ross (1994) identify nine elements that should receive attention in a comprehensive instructional [development] plan:

1. Identify *instructional problems,* and specify goals for designing an instructional program.

2. Examine *learner characteristics* that should receive attention during planning.

3. Identify *subject content,* and analyze *task* components related to stated goals and purposes.

4. State *instructional objectives* for the learner.

5. *Sequence content* within each instructional unit for logical learning.

6. Design *instructional strategies* so that each learner can master the objectives.

7. Plan *instructional delivery* within three patterns for teaching and learning.

8. Develop *evaluation* instruments to assess objectives.

9. Select *resources* to support instruction and learning activities. (p. 8-9)

Kemp, Morrison and Ross suspect that ID is a continuous cycle and that revision is an on-going activity associated with all the other elements. They suspect the teacher/designer can start anywhere and proceed in any order. This is essentially a general system view of development wherein all elements are interdependent, and may be performed independently or simultaneously as appropriate.

Although Kemp, Morrison and Ross indicate in their model that the developer can start anywhere, their narrative presents the model in a conventional framework starting with topics, job tasks, and purposes. The classroom orientation of their model is apparent through their choice of the words, "topics," and "subject content" for determining what will be taught. These words can readily be accepted by classroom teachers. From a teacher's perspective, the strength of this model lies in the concept of starting "where you are." The emphasis on subject matter content, goals and purposes, and selection of resources also makes it attractive to teachers. The version of the model reviewed here is different from the one reviewed in earlier editions of this monograph. The current version places greater emphasis on both formative and summative evaluation as ongoing processes, and places all activities within the context of goals, priorities, and constraints. This model is one of the very few that has been modified over time.

The Heinich, Molenda, Russell and Smaldino Model

Heinich, Molenda, Russell and Smaldino (1996) present their classroom oriented instructional development model (ASSURE) in what is currently the most widely distributed college text on instructional media and technology. While some might argue that their model is not a complete or formal instructional development model, teachers can readily identify with the planning process it describes, and its wide circulation alone would warrant its inclusion in this review. Unlike most ID models, ASSURE is not portrayed in graphic or pictorial form. ASSURE is an acronym for

A   analyze learners

S   state objectives

S   select media and materials

U   utilize materials

R   require learner participation

E   evaluation/review

The **A,** for *Analyze Learners,* acknowledges the importance of determining the entry characteristics of learners. Heinich, Molenda, Russell and Smaldino caution teachers that it is not feasible to analyze all learner attributes. They suggest that only selected "general characteristics" (e.g., grade level, job or position, and cultural and economic factors) and selected specific entry competencies (e.g., knowledge, technical vocabulary, attitudes, and misconceptions) be examined. They also suggest that "learning style" (anxiety, aptitude, visual and auditory preference, etc.) be considered, but acknowledge problems of defining and measuring these characteristics. Their second step, **S,** for *State Objectives,* places emphasis on the requirement that desired outcomes of instruction be stated in specific and measurable terms. A rationale for stating measurable objectives is present-

41

ed, including the role of objectives in strategy and media selection, assessment of learning, and communicating the intent of the instruction to learners.

The second **S** in their model, *Select Media and Materials*, acknowledges that most teachers have little time for designing and developing their own materials. However, Heinich, Molenda, Russell and Smaldino do discuss the option of modifying existing materials, and indicate that sometimes original development may be possible. The procedures and criteria they present for selecting media and materials provide useful guidelines to teachers and to those assisting teachers in that task. The **U**, or *Utilize Materials*, step in the Heinich, Molenda, Russell and Smaldino model discusses how teachers need to plan how to use the selected media and materials in the classroom. The practical advice they offer recognizes the realities of most American classrooms and the fact that teachers play a central role in delivering most instruction. The **R**, *Require Learner Participation*, step in the ASSURE model emphasizes the importance of keeping learners actively involved. The role of feedback and practice are also described. While one might question why learner participation is singled out (over other design considerations) to be a step in the ASSURE model, Heinich, Molenda, Russell and Smaldino consider learner participation to be of primary importance. The last step in their model, **E**, *Evaluation/Review*, is in reality two steps—evaluation and review. They discuss the importance of evaluating the "total picture" to assure both learner achievement of the objectives, and the feasibility of the instructional process itself. Review is then planned based on discrepancies between intended and actual outcomes.

Although Heinich, Molenda, Russell and Smaldino's model focuses on media and materials selection and utilization, in contrast to a wider view of the ID process, their model has much to offer classroom teachers. The relationship of its steps to an authentic environment, and the model's practical guidance and structure, make it easy to understand and apply. The well written text and accompanying teacher's manual are also excellent resources for teaching teachers the rudiments of the ID process.

The Reiser and Dick Model

Reiser and Dick (1996) present both an outline for an instructional design, and a development model for preparing and implementing the design. However, they have adopted the term *instructional planning* in lieu of either design or development. This decision is consistent with research on strategies for preparing teachers as instructional designers (Earle, in press). Reiser and Dick offer the model depicted in Figure 9, and suggest that teachers and others involved in instructional planning adhere to the following four principles as they apply the model:

1. Begin the planning process by clearly identifying the general goals and specific objectives students will be expected to attain;

2. Plan instructional activities that are intended to help students attain those objectives;

3. Develop assessment instruments that measure attainment of those objectives; and

4. Revise instruction in light of student performance on each objective and student attitudes towards your instructional activities. (p. 4)

Reiser and Dick's model and accompanying narrative are straightforward and easy to comprehend. The process they describe is influenced by their experience and expertise in educational psychology, measurement, and evaluation. Their instructional planning model is presented in a chapter format familiar to teachers. Each chapter includes:

*   *Problem Scenario*: a description of a common teaching situation. The scenario provides a familiar theme for subsequent instructional planning activities.

*   *Chapter Objectives*: stated in terms of what one will be able to do as a result of having read and studied the chapter.

*   *Background Information*: includes information that bridges the chap-

ters and locates the procedures within a larger framework. A theoretical perspective is sometimes described.

- *Major Concepts and Examples*: ideas and concepts are presented with accompanying examples demonstrating application. Improper applications are also presented.

- *Practice and Feedback*: includes a variety of exercises directly related to the chapter objectives. Provides an opportunity to compare the reader's responses to the feedback in the text.

- *Application*: guides the reader in developing a specific portion of the instructional plan. By the time the reader finishes, he/she will have developed and evaluated an entire instructional plan.

- *Summary*: summarizes the major ideas presented. A glossary that contains definitions of some of the key terms is located at the back of the book.

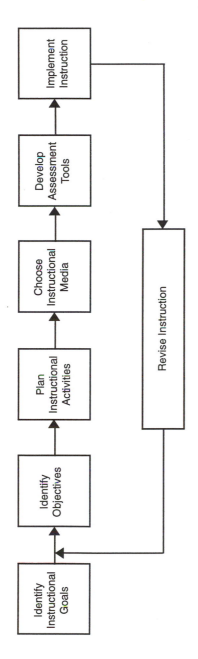

Figure 9. Reprinted from *Instructional planning: A guide for teachers* (second edition) by Reiser, R., & Dick, W. Copyright © 1996 by Allyn and Bacon. Reprinted/adapted by permission from Allyn and Bacon.

Chapter

4

Product Orientation

Assumptions

Product development models typically assume that the amount of product to be developed will be several hours, or perhaps several days, in length. The amount of front-end analysis for product oriented models may vary widely, but it is usually assumed that a technically sophisticated product will be produced.

Users may have no contact with the developers. Product development models are characterized by four key features:

(1) product development models usually assume that the instructional product is needed;

(2) product development models assume something new will be produced, rather than selected or modified from existing materials;

(3) product development models place considerable emphasis on tryout and revision; and

(4) product development models assume that the product must be usable by a variety of "managers" or facilitators of instruction.

The assumption of need should not necessarily be considered a limitation of these models. In some settings, a front-end analysis has already been conducted, and needs already determined for a variety of products. The task then becomes the development of the products efficiently and effectively. Often the need is so obvious, that it is unnecessary to ask "should," but only "what" should be done. An example would be the necessity to develop an operator training package for a new machine that is about to be marketed.

Extensive tryout and revision often accompany product development because the end-user cannot, or will not, tolerate low performance. Also, the performance level may be externally established, such as the user being able to utilize all the capabilities of word processing software. This is in contrast to classroom settings where the performance level is often subject to considerable up or down adjustment based on the effectiveness of the instruction. Cosmetic appearance of the product may also be important to clients, thus making subjective evaluation an important part of the tryout process. Use of the product by managers, as opposed to teachers, usually means the product is often required to stand on its own without a content expert available next to the learner. An example would be training for a telephone company line engineer on how to install a specialized piece of equipment. The demand for free standing products is another reason why tryout and revision are emphasized in product development. As computer-based instruction has become more popular, the demand for effective instructional products has increased, and that demand is likely to expand even more rapidly in the future. The demand for highly prescriptive ID models, applicable to a variety of settings and instructional products, is therefore likely to continue and increase.

Products models often contain elements that might qualify them as systems models (which we will discuss in the next section). The three instructional product models chosen for this review were selected based on our belief that they are primarily focused on creating instructional products rather than more comprehensive instruction systems. The three models we will discuss are: Van Patten (1989); Leshin, Pollock, and Reigeluth (1990); and Bergman & Moore (1990).

The Van Patten Model

Van Patten's model is described in a chapter he wrote for the book, *Instructional Design: New Alternatives for Effective Education & Training* edited by Johnson & Foa (1989). Van Patten's introduction to his model is a little confusing because he first talks about the instructional design process as performed by instructional designers to produce products. Later, he talks about the process as Instructional Systems Design (ISD).

The ISD model (Figure 10) Van Patten presents and describes can be, according to Van Patten, used to create paper-based instructional materials. It has nine phases each having a deliverable, one or more persons responsible for its execution, and one or more persons responsible for its evaluation. The nine phases are: *Analysis, Design, Development, Pilot test, Review, Production, Duplication, Implementation,* and *Maintenance.* Analysis includes defining the problem, identifying the audience, determining resources, and specifying the goals of the effort. The *Design* phase involves preparing the "floor plan" and "pen and ink" renderings of design specifications. The *Development* phase has four sub-phases: developing

Phase	Deliverable	Created by	Evaluated by
Analysis	Analysis Report	Designer/Evaluator	Client
Design	Specification	Designer	Client/SME
Development	Draft materials	Developer/Designer	Client/SME
Pilot test	Test results	Designer/Evaluator	Client/SME
Revision	Final materials	Developer/Editor	Client/SME
Production	Camera-ready	Editor/Graphics	Client/SME
Duplication	Inventory	Graphics/Printer	Client/Administrator
Implementation	Training begins	Instructor/Administrator	Client
Maintenance	Periodic Evaluations	Instructor/Designer Administrator/Evaluator	Client

Figure 10. Reprinted from *Instructional design: New alternatives for effective education and training* by Johnson, K. A. & Foa, L. J.   Copyright © 1989 by the American Council on Education/Macmillan Publishing Company.   Copyright © 1994 by the American Council on Education and The Oryx Press. Used with permission from the American Council on Education and The Oryx Press, 4041 N. Central Ave., Suite 700, Phoenix, AZ 85012. (800) 279-6799.

definitions of each topic, developing examples for each definition, developing practice exercises for the examples, and developing "everything else." Phases four and five, *Pilot test* and *Review*, are described together as an interactive loop that is repeated until the instruction is judged "good enough." Phase six, *Production*, is the step at which all materials are put through final production and prepared for duplication. *Duplication*, phase seven, is essentially the task of building an inventory of material in preparation for distribution. Phases eight and nine, *Implementation and Maintenance*, are described together as an interactive loop that takes place as long as the product continues to be used.

Van Patten's model is similar to other product models in that it specifies extensive tryout (pilot test and review) before the product is finalized. It also specifies implementation and maintenance, activities not always associated with product development. If the product is publicly marketed, no formal implementation or maintenance (in Van Patten's use of the terms) would likely occur. Van Patten's model is quite serviceable as a general guide, but its lack of operational detail limits its use to those already familiar with specific procedures for performing the activities described.

The Leshin, Pollock and Reigeluth Model

Leshin, Pollock and Reigeluth (1990) claim they have developed a model (Figure 11) that redresses the shortcomings of other models that, "have not included any guidance for the selection and use of instructional strategies and tactics" (p.1). While we, in this survey, promote a somewhat contrary perspective, their point is well taken. Many models emphasize the analysis side of activities, with the actual design of instruction receiving considerably less attention. Leshin, Pollock and Reigeluth's model is significantly influenced by earlier work of Reigeluth and others (Reigeluth, 1980, 1983, 1992) and recent developments in cognitive psychology. Although the graphic representation of their model appears to be linear, they emphasize the cyclical and non-linear nature of their development process in the accompanying narrative.

51

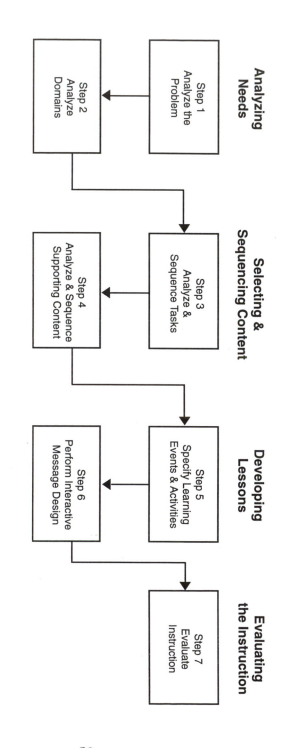

Figure 11. Reprinted from *Instructional design: Strategies and tactics for improving learning and performance* by Leshin, C., Pollock, J., & Reigeluth, C. Copyright © 1992 by Educational Technology Publications. Reprinted by permission of Educational Technology Publications.

Leshin, Pollock, and Reigeluth's model contains seven steps that are clustered under four headings: *Analyzing Needs, Selecting and Sequencing Content, Developing Lessons,* and *Evaluating the Instruction.* Step one is to *Analyze* the problem which can be a performance deficiency in a training situation, or simply a lack of knowledge in an educational setting. Identifying the audience, clearly stating the problem, determining possible solutions, and communicating the results are all part of this first step. Step two, *Analyze Domains,* contains four sub components: identify tasks, identify performance deficiencies, write performance objectives, and develop performance measures. Step three, *Analyze and Sequence* tasks, contains eight components not discussed in detail in this review, but heavily influenced by elaboration theory. Step four, *Analyze and Sequence Supporting Content,* is also based on Reigeluth's earlier work and provides considerable detail on how to perform these tasks. Step five, *Specify Learning Events and Activities,* involves classifying each piece of content as to type of learning, planning instructional "strategies and tactics," writing practice and test items, and specifying the instructional management plan. Step six, *Perform Interactive Message Design,* is really an examination of five alternate delivery systems along with a set of general considerations for message design. Step seven, *Evaluation,* consists of three components: one-on-one evaluation, pilot testing, and summative evaluation via field testing.

Leshin, Pollock, and Reigeluth have created a seven step model that specifically addresses their belief that greater attention should be paid to what some have called the psychological components of instructional design. Leshin, Pollock, and Reigeluth present numerous "job aids" to guide the development process. These job aids will be of considerable assistance to novice instructional developers.

The Bergman and Moore Model

Bergman and Moore (1990) published a model (Figure 12) intended to guide and manage the production of "Interactive Video/Multimedia"

The Development Model

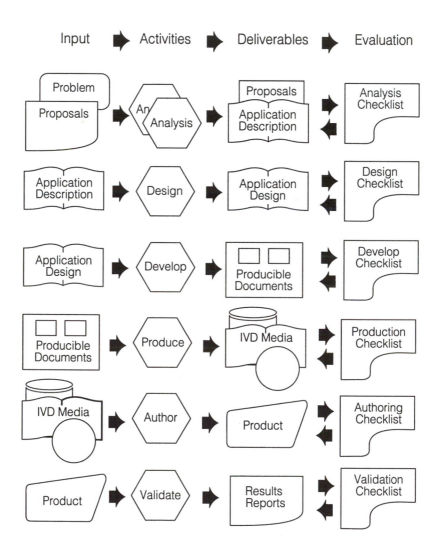

Figure 12. Reprinted from *Managing interactive video/multimedia projects* by Bergman, R.E. & Moore, T.V. Copyright © 1990 by Educational Technology Publications. Reprinted with permission of Educational Technology Publications.

products. Their model focuses on one of the current areas of keen interest in education and training technology. Although their model includes specific reference to interactive video (IVD) and multi-media (MM) products, it is generally applicable to a variety of "high-tech," interactive instructional products. Bergman and Moore's model is similar to the Control Data Corporation model (Gustafson, 1981) and other ID models that focused on the then current "high technology."

Bergman and Moore's model contains six major activities: *Analysis, Design, Develop, Production, Author,* and *Validate*. Each activity specifies input, deliverables (output), and evaluation strategies. The output of each activity provides the input for a subsequent activity. They refer to each horizontal row of their model as a "phase," and remind the reader that, although not shown, it may be necessary to review a phase and review selected activities. Bergman and Moore also emphasize the importance of evaluating the output (deliverable) from each activity before proceeding. The checklists they provide for performing these evaluations are extensive, and would be valuable even if one were using a different product development model for IVD or MM development.

Bergman and Moore claim that a request for proposal (RFP) initiates the development process. They suggest that even if an external RFP does not exist, preparing an internal RFP is desirable. The RFP drives *Analysis* activities including identification of the audience, tasks, user environments, and content. *Design* activities include sequencing the major segments and defining their treatment; labeled by Bergman and Moore "High-Level Design." Detailed design then follows, and includes specification of motivational elements, media, interaction strategies, and assessment methodology. *Development* includes preparing all the documents necessary for later production. Examples of what Bergman and Moore call "Producible Documents" are storybooks, audio scripts, shot lists, art and graphics renditions, and a database for managing production. *Production* "transforms the producible documentation into its corresponding medium: video sequence, audio, graphic, or text" (p. 17).

Authoring activities integrate the individual media into the completed product. Its three sub-activities involve coding, testing, and tuning. *Validation* consists of comparing the finished product with its original objectives. Revision, to reflect changing conditions or to increase effectiveness, may also occur at this time, as can assessing achievement of the product sponsor's goals.

Development of sophisticated IVD and MM products almost always requires a team, a point made repeatedly by Bergman and Moore. Interactive video and multimedia also require a sound management system, for which this model provides the structure. Bergman and Moore's model was selected for this review partially because of its focus on new technology, and partially because of the excellent and extensive checklists and other guides contained in the text. Even without the model, the support materials are well worth examining.

Chapter

5

System Orientation

Assumptions

System oriented models typically assume that a large amount of instruction, such as an entire course or entire curriculum, will be developed and that substantial resources will be made available to a team of highly trained developers. Assumptions as to whether original production or selection of materials will occur vary, but in many cases original development is specified. Assumptions about the technological sophistication of the delivery system vary, with trainers often opting for much more technology than teachers.

57

The amount of front-end analysis is usually high as is the amount of try-out and revision. Dissemination is usually quite wide, and typically does not involve the team that did the development.

Systems oriented ID models usually begin with a data collection phase to determine the feasibility and desirability of developing an instructional solution to a "problem." A number of systems oriented models require that a problem be specified in a given format before proceeding. Thomas Gilbert's (1978) and Mager and Pipe's (1984) work in front-end analysis is relevant to the models discussed here. These authors take the position that, although a problem may have an instructional solution, one should first consider lack of motivation on the part of the learner and environmental factors as alternative domains for action. Systems models, as a class, differ from product development models in the amount of emphasis placed on analysis of the larger environment before committing to development. Systems models also typically assume a larger scope of effort than product development models. However, in the design, development, and evaluation phases, the primary difference between systems models and product models is one of magnitude rather than type of specific tasks to be performed. We have selected six models to represent the variety of ID models most applicable in the systems environment: Instructional Development Institute (IDI) (National Special Media Institute, 1971), Interservices Procedures for Instructional Systems Development (IPISD) Branson (1975), Diamond (1997), Smith and Ragan (1993), Gentry (1994), and Dick and Carey (1996).

The IDI Model

The idea of presenting an ID model at different levels of detail formed the basis for a teacher training package known as the Instructional Development Institute (IDI). The Instructional Development Institute model (Figure 13) was a joint effort of the members of the University Consortium for Instructional Development and Technology (UCIDT), which was originally known as the National Special Media Institute. The

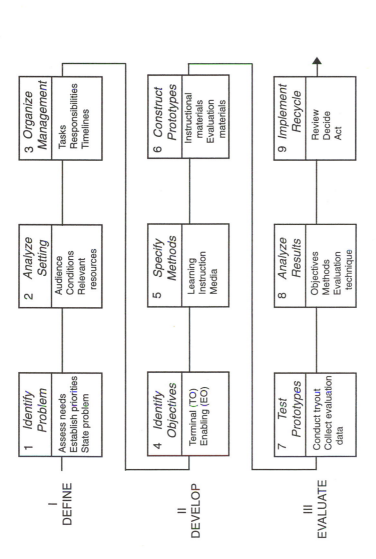

Figure 13. The Instructional Development Institute (IDI) model (National Special Media Institute, 1971). More recently known as the University Consortium for Instructional Development and Technology. Public domain document.

IDI model has three phases: *Define, Develop,* and *Evaluate,* each of which is broken into three steps, of which each is further broken into two or three elements. This seven (later reduced to five) day training program was created by a team from four universities [Michigan State University, Syracuse University, University of Southern California and United States International University]. Workshops were conducted with over 20,000 teachers in the late 1960s and early 1970s. Twelker, et al. (1972), used the IDI model as the frame of reference when he analyzed other models. The IDI model is problem oriented, specifies team development, and assumes distribution or dissemination of the results of the effort. It is similar in a number of its steps to an earlier model created by Dale Hamreus (1968), and some developers consider it simply a variation on his model.

The IDI model is essentially linear in its approach. The claim is briefly made that ID can be non-linear, but the procedures accompanying the graphic model provide no evidence of how this can be accomplished. The model has three stages and nine steps, with each step further sub-divided for a total of 24 elements. In essence, the model is conceived as being useful at all three levels of detail—stages, steps, or elements.

The model is reviewed at its intermediate level of detail because describing it at the 24-element level would result in too lengthy a description for this survey. The IDI's first step is to identify the problem. This requires conducting a needs assessment, establishing priorities among various and conflicting needs, and, finally, stating one or more problems to be addressed. Emphasis is placed on separating symptoms from problems, and stating problems in measurable terms. This permits later assessment of progress toward alleviating or solving the stated problems. Step two (analyze the setting) specifies additional data collection to be performed regarding the previously stated problem. Data are collected concerning audience (learner) characteristics, characteristics of other affected personnel, conditions under which development should occur, constraints on any solution, and what relevant material and human resources are available for both developing and delivering the solution.

Step three (organize management) is concerned with organization of the development team. This step is somewhat unique to the IDI model. Its creators made this step highly visible because of their belief that poor management often leads to failure of development efforts. Organizing management includes stating all major tasks, assigning responsibility for those tasks to team members, and establishing timelines for their completion. Monitoring of progress is also included as part of this step. How a team is to perform steps one and two before becoming organized is never explained.

Step four (identify objectives) is similar to other models in that it requires behaviorally stated objectives. The mnemonic ABCD provides a helpful reminder that objectives must include an Audience (A), Behavior (B), Condition (C), and Degree of performance (D). Step five (specify methods) uses a taxonomy developed by Edling and Hamreus, later modified by Merrill and Goodman (1970), for classifying objectives, and then selecting strategies and media based on the type of objective. The strategies and media prescription matrix is viewed as a set of suggestions, rather than a rigid matching activity. Designers and developers are encouraged to use whatever additional knowledge they have to make final determinations.

Step six (construct a prototype) prescribes the building of testable drafts of all materials. These include instructional units, teacher/manager instructions, and evaluation materials. The emphasis is on constructing a prototype that is complete enough to test, but not so expensive that it cannot be changed. The seventh step specifies testing the prototype under conditions as similar as possible to its eventual use. This step is often called formative evaluation in other models. Step eight specifies analyzing the results in terms of learner achievement, effectiveness and practicability of the methods of instruction, and appropriateness of the evaluation techniques. The last step in the IDI model is to recycle (if the data indicate a deficiency) or to implement the solution if it is effective. Recycling to any previous step should be considered, but it may be necessary to return to the original problem and re-analyze needs. In later years, the UCIDT Consortium developed a workshop on dissemination that is an extension of the model to another step, but the original model was not modified.

The basic strength of the IDI model is its three levels of detail. This permits its initial presentation to non-developers in a simple form that can be elaborated as their knowledge increases. The IDI model's basic limitation is the implication of a linear step-by-step development process beginning with definition of a problem. This limitation is common to many systems models. The IDI model's processes are also becoming dated due to lack of refinement since its introduction.

The IPISD Model

The Interservices Procedures for Instructional Systems Development (IPISD) model is, as the name suggests, a joint effort of the United States military services. The Army, Navy, Marines and Air Force created this model (Figure 14) in the interest of utilizing a common approach to instructional development. The motivation was to facilitate shared development efforts, and improve communication with contractors doing instructional development across different branches of the military. The underlying concern of each service was to have a rigorous procedure for developing effective instruction. A large number of personnel contributed to creating the IPISD model. However, the name most commonly associated with this model is Robert Branson.

Similar to the IDI model, the IPISD model has several levels of detail. The simplest level has five phases: *Analyze, Design, Develop, Implement,* and *Control.* These phases sub-divide into 20 steps which can be further divided into hundreds of sub-steps. In fact, the IPISD model is one of the most highly detailed models of the ID process generally available. It is published as a four volume set (Branson, 1975) and can be ordered from the National Technical Information Service (NTIS) or from the Educational Resources Information Center (ERIC).

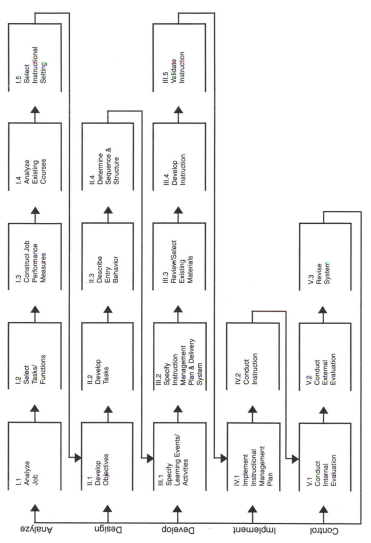

Figure 14. Reprinted from *Interservice procedures for instructional systems development: Executive summary and model* by Branson, R.K. (1975). Tallahassee, Florida: Center for Educational Technology, Florida State University. (National Technical Information Service, 5285 Port Royal Rd., Springfield, VA 22161. Document Nos. AD-A019, 486 to AD-A019 490.) Public domain document.

Because a detailed review of all the steps in this model is beyond the scope of this survey, we will review it only at the phase level. The reader should keep in mind that the IPISD approach is designed specifically for military training. Most other models have a much broader range of intended applications. The narrower focus of IPISD is both a blessing and a bane. Its virtue is the extremely detailed level of specification it contains. However, the price of this specification is the lack of generalizability of many of its specific procedures to other environments.

Phase one of IPISD (analyze) requires specification of the tasks military personnel perform on the job. Tasks which are already known or easy to acquire are subtracted, and a list of tasks requiring instruction is generated. Performance levels and evaluation procedures are specified for the tasks, and existing courses are examined to determine if any of the identified tasks are included. A decision is then made either to modify the existing course to fulfill task requirements, or to plan a new course. In the latter case, parts of an existing course may be adapted for the new one. The final step in phase one is to determine the most appropriate site for instruction; i.e., school or non-resident instruction.

Phase two (design) begins with the arrangement of job tasks into instructional outcomes classified by the learning elements involved; such as mental abilities, physical skills, information, and attitudes. Tests are generated and validated on a sample of the population, and instructional objectives are written in behavioral form. Next, the entry behavior expected of typical students is determined, followed by the design of the sequence and structure for the course. Design specifications are then forwarded to phase three of the process.

The development of prototype materials occurs in phase three of the model. Development begins by specifying a list of events and activities for inclusion in instruction. Media are then selected and a course management plan is developed. Existing instructional materials are reviewed for their relevance and, if appropriate, adopted or adapted for the course.

Necessary new materials are then produced, and the entire package is field tested and revised until satisfactory learner performance and system performance are achieved. The development phase concludes when the entire course package is ready for large scale implementation as phase four of the model.

Phase four (implement) includes training for course managers on how to use the package, content training of subject matter personnel, and distribution of all materials to the selected sites. Instruction is then conducted, and evaluation data is collected on both learner and system performance.

Phase five (control) is the last phase of the IPISD model. Internal evaluation is performed by "on-line" staff who are expected to make small-scale changes to improve the system after each offering. The on-line staff also forward evaluation results to a central location. External evaluation is a team effort directed toward identifying major deficiencies requiring immediate correction. External evaluation also follows course graduates to the job site to assess real-world performance. Changes in practice in the field are also monitored to determine necessary revisions to the course. Thus, the emphasis in phase five is on quality control and continued relevance of the training over an extended period of time.

The major strength of the IPISD model is its extensive specification of procedures to follow during the ID process. Its major limitations are its narrow instructional focus and its linear approach to ID. Further, the level of analysis and prescription it specifies could be done only by a heavily staffed, highly financed organization. Use of this model requires a commitment of substantial resources on a long-term basis. The IPISD model will find little use outside the military, the government, and a few large corporations having major job training programs. Nonetheless, it is an excellent reference for students who are in training to become instructional developers. Berkowitz and O'Neil (1979) prepared an annotated bibliography of additional relevant resources for the IPISD model.

The Diamond Model

Robert Diamond (1989, 1997) developed, and refined over a number of years, an instructional development model that is specific to higher education institutions (Figure 15). Although Diamond's model might be considered classroom oriented, we have placed it in the systems category because Diamond believes that development is a team effort and is often directed at total curricula in addition to individual courses. Diamond also emphasizes the need for developers to be sensitive to political and social issues existing on campus and within academic departments. Assuring that the proposed development effort is consistent with organizational priorities and missions is another critical concern for Diamond. He believes ID is a team process with significant input from university personnel specifically assigned to assist faculty with ID. For these reasons, Diamond's model seems most appropriate for classification as a systems model.

Diamond's model is divided into two phases: *Project Selection and Design,* and *Production, Implementation, and Evaluation.* During phase one, the feasibility and desirability of launching the project are examined. Instructional issues such as enrollment projections and level of effectiveness of existing courses, as well as institutional priorities and faculty enthusiasm, are all considered prior to beginning development. Diamond recommends beginning the ID process by thinking in terms of an "ideal" solution without regard to existing constraints. His argument is that by thinking in ideal terms, a team will be more creative and innovative in outlining powerful solutions. Once a decision is made to begin a project, an operational plan is developed that accounts for the goals, timeline, human and other resources, and student needs.

During phase two of development, each unit of the course or curriculum proceeds through a seven-step process. The first step is to determine the unit's objectives. This is followed by design of evaluation instruments and procedures, a step that proceeds concurrently with selecting the instructional format and examining existing materials for their possible inclusion in the system. Once these steps have been accomplished, any necessary

66

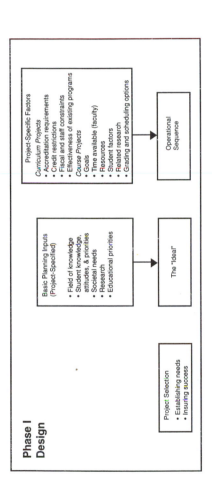

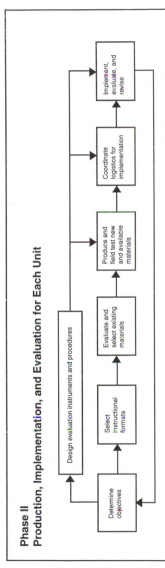

Figure 15. Reprinted from *Designing and assessing courses and curricula: A practical guide* by Diamond, R.M. (1997). San Francisco, California: Jossey-Bass. In press. Copyright © 1998 by author. Reprinted with permission of author.

new materials are produced and modifications are made to any materials that exist, but require modification. Interestingly, Diamond includes field testing as part of the same step as materials production, although most model developers make them separate steps. Also implicit to this step is revision of the unit based on field test data, but Diamond also includes revision later in the process. The next to the last step is coordinating logistics for implementation, followed by full scale implementation including evaluation and revision.

Diamond emphasizes that developers should match decisions on whether to engage in instructional development to institutional missions as well as to instructional issues. He stresses the need to assure faculty ownership of the results of the development effort, and the need for a formal organization to support faculty's development efforts.

The Smith and Ragan Model

Patricia Smith and Tim Ragan (1993) created an instructional design process model (Figure 16) that is becoming increasingly popular for students and professionals in the field of instructional technology who are interested in the cognitive psychology base of the ID process. For this reason, almost half of the procedures in their process address the design of instructional strategies. Smith and Ragan accommodate the paradigm shift from previous views of systems and behaviorist concepts, but retain the general systems model for instructional design, and the specification of learner outcomes, prior to initiating the instructional development process.

Smith and Ragan's model has three phases: Analyzing the Learning Context, Generating Instructional Strategies, and Formative and Summative Evaluation. These three phases provide the conceptual framework for the eight steps that comprise their ID process. Their eight-step approach includes: *Analyzing the Learning Context, Analyzing the Learners, Analyzing the Learning Task, Assessing Learner Performance, Develop*

68

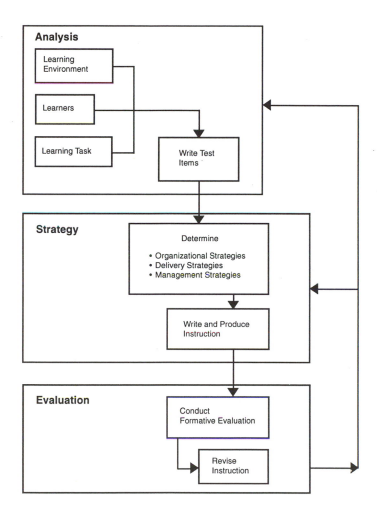

Figure 16. Reprinted from *Instructional design* by Smith, P. L., & Ragan, T.J., Copyright © 1992. Reprinted by permission of Prentice-Hall, Inc., Upper Saddle River, NJ.

Instructional Strategies, Produce Instruction, Conduct Evaluation, and *Revise Instruction.* Analyzing the learner is a two-part procedure: (1) substantiation of a need for instruction in a certain content area, and (2) description of the learning environment in which the instructional product will be used. *Analyzing the Learners* suggests procedures for describing the stable and changing characteristics of the intended learner audience. *Analyzing the Learning Task* outlines procedures for recognizing and writing appropriate instructional goals. *Assessing Learner Performance* specifies procedures for identifying which of several possible assessment items are valid assessments of objectives for various types of learning. *Develop Instructional Strategies* is the step that offers strategies for organizing and managing instruction. *Produce Instruction* is the step that offers strategies for translating the decisions and specifications made in previous steps into instructional materials and trainer guides. *Formative and Summative Evaluation* is the step that specifies procedures for evaluating the effectiveness of the instructional materials during development and after implementation. *Revise Instruction* outlines procedures for modifying the proposed instruction.

The Smith and Ragan model reflects principles associated with: the systematic process, problem solving orientations, learner-centered instruction, goal-oriented instruction, instructional alignment, and theoretical and empirical foundations. Their model is valuable for introducing the philosophy and theory of the systematic design of instruction to practitioners new to the field as well as to people who study within the field.

The Gentry IPDM Model

Castelle Gentry (1994) presents an Instructional Project Development and Management (IPDM) model that is designed to introduce the concepts and procedures of the ID process and the supporting processes (Figure 17). His model attends to *what* needs to be done and *how* something should be done during an instructional development project. Gentry's model is accompanied by techniques and job aids for completing the tasks associated with instructional development. While, according to Gentry, his model is intended for graduate students, practicing instructional developers, and teachers, his comprehensive description of the entire process and the accompanying tools for managing large projects, make it suitable for developing large-scale systems.

Gentry's model is divided into two groups of components: *Development Components* and *Supporting Components*. A *Communication Component* connects the two clusters. There are eight *Development Components:*

(1) Needs Analysis: establish needs and prioritize goals for existing or proposed instruction;

(2) Adoption: establish acceptance by decision makers, and obtain commitment of resources;

(3) Design: specify objectives, strategies, techniques, and media;

(4) Production: construct project elements specified by the design and revision data;

(5) Prototyping: assemble, pilot test, validate, and finalize an instructional unit;

(6) Installation: establish the necessary conditions for effective operation of a new instructional product;

(7) Operation: maintain the instructional product after its installation; and

(8) Evaluation: collect, analyze, and summarize data to enable revision decisions.

There are five *Supporting Components:*

(1) Management: process by which resources are controlled, coordinated, integrated, and allocated to accomplish project goals;

71

(2) Information Handling: process of selecting, collecting, generating, organizing, storing, retrieving, distributing, and assessing information required by an ID project;

(3) Resource Acquisition and Allocation: process of determining resource requirements, formalizing budgets, and acquiring and distributing resources;

(4) Personnel: process of determining staffing requirements, hiring, training, assessing, motivating, counseling, censuring, and dismissing ID project members; and

(5) Facilities: process for organizing and renovating spaces for design, implementation, and testing of elements of instruction.

The IPDM model brings significant attention to the importance of sharing information between the two clusters of components during the life of the instructional development project. The communication component is the "process by which essential information is distributed and circulated among those responsible for, or involved in, the activities of a project" (Gentry, 1994, p. 5).

A unique quality of Gentry's IPDM model is the way the instructional development process is related to specific techniques for implementing the process. Some may view the IPDM model as a somewhat mechanistic approach to instructional development because of its reliance on jargon and its behavioristic orientation. However, the model depicts procedures that contain enough descriptive and prescriptive information, and at varying levels of detail, to make Gentry's model a source for a comprehensive introduction to the processes and techniques of instructional development.

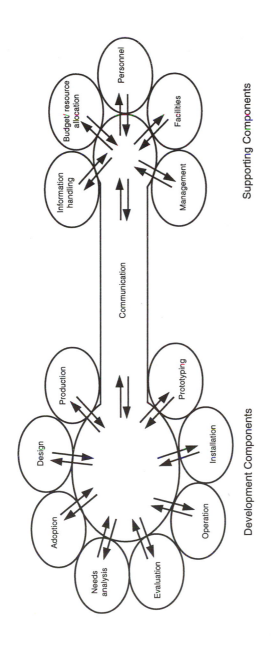

Figure 17. Reprinted from *Introduction to instructional development process and technique* by Gentry, C. G. Copyright © 1994 by the Wadsworth Publishing Company, a Division of Wadsworth, Inc. Reprinted by permission of Wadsworth Publishing Company.

73

The Dick and Carey Model

Walter Dick and Lou Carey (1996) have produced one of the most widely used introductory texts and accompanying model (Figure 18) for instructional development. The Dick and Carey model might be considered product oriented rather than system oriented, depending on the size and scope of step one activities (Identify Instructional Goals). Many of the examples and worksheets seem to be directed at developing specific instructional products, but parts of the narrative suggest a more encompassing perspective. For our purposes, we consider the Dick and Carey model to be a systems model that is also applicable to projects having a more limited focus. It should also be noted that Dick and Carey use the term instructional design for the overall process that we define as instructional development.

Dick and Carey's model begins with *Assess Needs to Identify Goal(s)*. The first component of their model immediately distinguishes it from many other instructional development models by promoting needs assessment procedures. Dick and Carey recommend criteria for establishing instructional goals as a way to decide what one is trying to achieve before beginning the ID process. Two steps are then conducted in parallel: *Conduct Instructional Analysis* and *Analyze Learners and Contexts*. The former is vintage hierarchical analysis as conceived by Gagné, with procedures added for constructing cluster analysis diagrams for verbal information. The latter step specifies collecting information about prospective learners' knowledge, skills and attitudes, and information about the environment in which they are situated. The next step is *Write Performance Objectives* in measurable terms, followed by *Developing Assessment Instruments*. Criterion-referenced test items are generated for each objective. *Develop Instructional Strategy* is the step that recommends ways to develop strategies for assisting a particular group of learners to achieve a set of objectives. The next step is *Develop and Select Instructional Materials*. Dick and Carey acknowledge the desirability of selecting, as well as developing materials, but the degree of emphasis they devote to development suggests they are far more interested in original development. The next step is *Design and Conduct Formative Evaluation*, a process for which they give

74

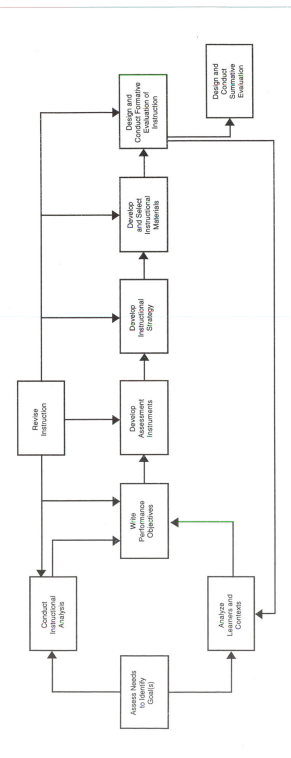

Figure 18. Reprinted from *The systematic design of instruction*, 4th Edition by Dick, W. & Carey, L. Copyright © 1996 by Walter Dick and Lou Carey. Reprinted by permission of Addison-Wesley Educational Publishers, Inc.

excellent guidance. *Revision* is the step that outlines various methods for collecting, summarizing, and analyzing data collected during the ID process that can be used to facilitate revision decisions. *Design and Conduct Summative Evaluation* determines the degree to which the original instructional goals (and perhaps other unintended ones) have been achieved.

The Dick and Carey model reflects the fundamental instructional design process used in many business, industry, government, and military training settings, and also reflects the influence of performance technology and the application of computers to instruction. The Dick and Carey model is valuable for introducing the concepts and applications of the systematic design of instruction to people new to the field.

Chapter

6

Conclusions

After reading this review of representative instructional development models, you may be somewhat unsure about how you should react to the wide variety of models presented. The literature is replete with models, each claiming to be unique and deserving of attention. While there may be hundreds of ID models, there are few major distinctions among them. Many ID models are simply restatements of earlier models with somewhat different terminology. There is also a disturbingly small volume of literature describing any testing of the models. While no one can be certain, it is possible many have never been applied in practice, let alone rigorously evaluated.

The typical article mentioning an ID model simply describes its major steps or stages, and perhaps explains how the steps are to be performed. The authors usually assume their models are worthwhile, but many authors do not present evidence to substantiate their positions. In some instances, a case study of a development project may be presented along with a model, but even this rudimentary level of validation is less common than we would prefer.

We hope that in the future, at least some ID models will be subjected to rigorous scientific validation. Such validation would require precise description of the elements of the model, followed by systematic data collection concerning the application and impact of those elements. The investigator would also need to be alert to possible discrepant data not accounted for in the model. Repeated trials under such conditions would, if the model had validity, result in a precise set of findings regarding the conditions under which the model was valid. It is probably safe to say none of the models currently available in the literature has been subjected to such rigorous scrutiny. In fact, most authors completely ignore mentioning the conditions under which their models should be used. For a more complete discussion of procedures for validating a model, the reader is referred to an excellent chapter on models and modeling by Rubinstein (1975).

What then, should the response of the responsible ID professional be to the plethora of ID models described in the literature? First, we would suggest that the developer acquire a working knowledge of several models, and be certain that all three categories in our taxonomy are represented. As new and different models are encountered, the new models can then be compared to those with which the developer is familiar. Should a client bring a model to a development project, it is probably better for the developer to use it (modified if required) rather than force the client to adopt the developer's favorite model. We also suggest that developers maintain a repertoire of examples of ID models that can be presented to clients along with varying levels of detail. Such a repertoire will allow the developer to introduce the ID process to uninformed clients easily. More detailed information can be explained to the client later as development progresses. A developer should always be in the position of selecting an appropriate model to fit a situation, rather than forcing the situation to fit a model. As has been noted in other contexts, "If the only tool you have is a hammer, you tend to treat everything like a nail." Like all competent professionals, instructional developers should have a number of tools in their tool bags, and should select the right tools for the right job.

We cannot predict the future by looking back over trends in ID models since the publication of the last ERIC monograph in this series. There has been little substantive change in the general conceptual framework of ID models that suggests any trend. While some recent models (e.g., Bergman & Moore, 1990) focus on new delivery systems, these models do not represent new conceptions of the ID process. The only safe forecast based on the past would be that little change is likely to occur in the new few years. Walter Dick (1996), commenting on the possible obsolescence of the ID model he and Lou Carey have made so popular, thinks that it will survive well into the next century, and be able to accommodate new developments in theory and technology. We agree with Dick, not only about their model, but also about all the other models we reviewed in this survey.

We may be on the threshold of enhancements to several fundamental concepts related to the instructional development process. These enhancements will not result in the discarding of current concepts, but will significantly expand the range of possible approaches to developing instruction. We believe one of the profound changes will be a move away from the notion that education or training occurs in one environment, and performance occurs in another. In what promises to be an increasingly complex and dynamic world, information in the next decade will be far too abundant, and some of it much too transitory, to warrant formal instruction. Embedded instruction, expert systems to guide performance, microworlds, and an increased emphasis on learning how to learn and apply knowledge, will call for new design and development procedures that will be somewhat different from those depicted by current ID models.

Attempts to create automated systems for designing instruction (c.f., Spector, Polson, & Muraida, 1993; Li & Merrill, 1990) are having modest success to date, but do hold some promise for making at least parts of the development process more efficient. Rapid prototyping (Tripp & Bichelmeyer, 1990) holds promise as a procedure for developing certain forms of technology-based instruction. The highly iterative set of cycles used in rapid prototyping can, under some conditions, take the place of extensive analysis and design, and may also enhance creativity. Additional research on both automated design and rapid prototyping, plus practical application of these techniques, will determine just how useful they will prove to be. We must again emphasize that these, and other new ID approaches, will not replace existing procedures, but will become alternatives to them. For a more complete description of some of these new developments, we refer you to Briggs, Gustafson and Tillman (1991). Lastly, we invite you to prepare for an exciting and challenging decade ahead.

References

Andrews, D. H., & Goodson, L. A. (1980). A comparative analysis of models of instructional design. *Journal of Instructional Development, 3*(4), 2-16.

Association for Educational Communications and Technology. (1977). *Educational technology definition and glossary of terms.* Washington, DC: Author.

Barson, J. (1967, June) *Instructional systems development : A demonstration and evaluation project: Final report.* East Lansing, MI: Michigan State University. (ED 020 673)

Bergman, R., & Moore, T. (1990). *Managing interactive video/multimedia projects.* Englewood Cliffs, NJ: Educational Technology Publications.

Berkowitz, M., & O'Neil, H. (1979). *An annotated bibliography for instructional systems development.* Army Research Inst. for the Behavioral and Social Sciences, Alexandria, VA: ERIC Clearinghouse on Information and Technology. (ED 186 023)

Branch, R. (1997). Perceptions of instructional design process models. In R. E. Griffin, D. G. Beauchamp, J. M. Hunter, & C. B. Schiffman (Eds.), *Selected Readings of the 28th Annual Convention of the International Visual Literacy Association.* Cheyenne, WY.

Branson, R. K. (1975). *Interservice procedures for instructional systems development: Executive summary and model.* Tallahassee, FL: Center for Educational Technology, Florida State University. (National Technical Information Service, 5285 Port Royal Rd., Springfield, VA 22161. Document Nos. AD-A019, 486 to AD-A019 490)

Briggs, L. J., Gustafson, K. L., & Tillman, M. H. (Eds.). (1991).

Instructional design: Principles and applications, (2nd ed.). Englewood Cliffs, NJ: Educational Technology Publications.

Cohen, S. A., & Hyman, J. S. (1982, April). *Components of effective instruction*. Paper presented at the annual meeting of the American Educational Research Association. New York, NY.

Cruz, B. J. (1997). Measuring the transfer of training. *Performance Improvement Quarterly, 10*(2), 83-97.

Diamond, R. M. (1989). *Designing and improving courses and curricula in higher education.* San Francisco, CA: Jossey-Bass. (ED 304 056)

Diamond, R. M. (1997). *Designing and assessing courses and curricula: A practical guide.* San Francisco, CA: Jossey-Bass. In press.

Dick, W. (1996). The Dick and Carey model: Will it survive the decade? *Educational Technology Research and Development, 44*(3), 55-63. (EJ 532 854)

Dick, W., & Carey, L. (1996). *The systematic design of instruction* (4th ed.). New York: Harper Collins College Publishers.

Earle, R. (in press). Instructional design and teacher planning: Reflections and perspectives. In R. Branch, & M. Fitzgerald (Vol. Eds.), *Educational Media and Technology Yearbook*: Volume 23. Englewood, CO: Libraries Unlimited.

Edmonds, G., Branch, R., & Mukherjee, P. (1994). A conceptual framework for comparing instructional design models. *Educational Technology Research and Development, 42*(4), 55-62. (EJ 496 612)

Ely, D. (1973). Defining the field of educational technology. *Audiovisual Instruction, 8*(3), 52-53.

Ely, D. (1983). The definition of educational technology: An emerging stability. *Educational Considerations, 10*(2), 2-4.

Gagné, R. M., Briggs, L. J., & Wager, W. W. (1992). *Principles of instructional design* (4th Ed.). New York: Holt, Rinehart and Winston.

Gentry, C. G. (1994). *Introduction to instructional development: Process and technique.* Belmont, CA: Wadsworth Publishing Company.

Gerlach, V. S., & Ely, D. P. (1980). *Teaching and media: A systematic approach* (2nd ed.). Englewood Cliffs, NJ: Prentice-Hall Incorporated.

Gilbert, T. (1978). *Human competence: Engineering worthy performance.* New York: McGraw-Hill.

Greer, M. (1992). *ID project management: Tools and techniques for instructional designers and developers.* Englewood Cliffs, NJ: Educational Technology Publications.

Gustafson, K. L. (1981). *Survey of instructional development models.* Syracuse University: ERIC Clearinghouse on Information and Technology. (ED 211 097)

Gustafson, K. L. (1991). *Survey of instructional development models.* (2nd ed.) [with an annotated ERIC bibliography by G. C. Powell]. Syracuse University: ERIC Clearinghouse on Information and Technology. (ED 335 027)

Hamreus, D. (1968). *The systems approach to instructional development. The contribution of behavioral science to instructional technology.* Monmouth, OR: Oregon State System of Higher Education, Teaching Research Division. (ED 041 448)

Heinich, R., Molenda, M., Russell, J., & Smaldino, S. (1996). *Instructional media and technologies for learning* (5th ed.). New York: Macmillan.

Kemp, J. (1985). *The instructional design process.* New York: Harper & Row.

Kemp, J. E., Morrison, G. R., & Ross, S. M. (1994). *Designing effective instruction.* New York: Merrill.

Leshin, C., Pollock, J., & Reigeluth, C. (1992). *Instructional design: Strategies and tactics for improving learning and performance.* Englewood Cliffs, NJ: Educational Technology Publications.

Li, Z., & Merrill, M. D. (1990). Transaction shells: A new approach to courseware authoring. *Journal of Research on Computing in Education, 23*(1), 72-86. (EJ 415 357)

Mager, R., & Pipe, P. (1984). *Analyzing performance problems: Or you really oughta wanna.* Belmont, CA: Lake Publishing.

Markle, S. (1964). *Good frames and bad: A grammar of frame writing.* New York: Wiley. (ED 019 867)

Markle, S. (1978). *Designs for instructional designers.* Champaign, IL: Stipes Publishing Company.

Merrill, M. D., & Goodman, R. I. (1972). *Selecting instructional strategies and media: A place to begin.* National Special Media Institutes, Washington, DC: Bureau of Libraries and Educational Technology. (ED 111 391)

National Special Media Institute. (1971). *What is an IDI?* East Lansing, MI: Michigan State University.

Reigeluth, C. M. (1979). In search of a better way to organize instruction: The elaboration theory. *Journal of Instructional Development, 2*(3), 8-14. (EJ 222 015)

Reigeluth, C. M. (1983). Instructional design: What is it and why is it. In C. M. Reigeluth (Ed.). *Instructional design theories and models: An overview of their current status.* Hillsdale, NJ: Lawrence, Earlbaum Associates.

Reigeluth, C. M. (1992). Elaborating the elaboration theory. *Educational Technology Research and Development, 40*(3), 80-86. (EJ 462 855)

Reiser, R., & Dick, W. (1996). *Instructional Planning: A guide for teachers* (second edition). Boston: Allyn and Bacon.

Rowland, G. (1992). What do instructional designers actually do? An initial investigation of expert practice. *Performance Improvement Quarterly, 5*(2), 65-86. (EJ 446 270)

Rubinstein, M. (1975). *Patterns of problem solving.* Englewood Cliffs, NJ: Prentice-Hall.

Salisbury, D. (1990). General System Theory and Instructional System Design. *Performance and Instruction, 29*(2), 1-11. (EJ 408 935)

Seels, B., & Glasgow, Z. (1990). *Exercises in instructional design.* Columbus, OH: Merrill Publishing.

Seels, B., & Richey, R. (1994). *Instructional Technology: The definitions and domains of the field.* Washington, DC: Association for Educational Communications and Technology.

Silvern, L. C. (1965). *Basic analysis.* Los Angeles, CA: Education and Training Consultants Company.

Smith, P. L., & Ragan, T. J. (1993). *Instructional design.* New York: Macmillan.

Spector, J. M., Polson, P., & Muraida, D. (Eds.) (1993). *Automating instructional design: Concepts and issues.* Englewood Cliffs, NJ: Educational Technology Publications.

Stamas, S. (1973). A descriptive study of a synthesized model, reporting its effectiveness, efficiency, and cognitive and affective influence of the development process on a client. (Doctoral dissertation, Michigan State University, 1972). *Dissertation Abstracts International, 34,* (University Microfilms No 74-6139).

Tripp, S., & Bichelmeyer, B. (1990). Rapid prototyping: An alternative instructional design strategy. *Educational Technology Research & Development, 38*(1), 31-44. (EJ 412 118)

Twelker, et al. (1972). *The systematic development of instruction: An overview and basic guide to the literature.* Stanford, CA: Stanford University, ERIC Clearinghouse on Educational Media and Technology. (ED 059 629)

Van Patten, J. (1989). What is instructional design? In K. A. Johnson & L. K. Foa (Eds.), *Instructional design: New alternatives for effective education and training.* New York: Macmillan.

Wedman, J., & Tessmer, M. (1991). Adapting instructional design to project circumstance: The layers of necessity model. *Educational Technology, 31*(7), 48-52.

Zemke, R., & Kramlinger, T. (1984). *Figuring things out : A trainer's guide to needs and task analysis.* Reading, MA: Addison-Wesley.

Bibliography

ERIC Documents

Bohlin, R. M., & Milheim, W. D. (1994). Applications of an adult motivational instructional design model. In: *Proceedings of Selected Research and Development Presentations at the 1994 National Convention of the Association for Educational Communications and Technology Sponsored by the Research and Theory Division* (16th, Nashville, TN, February 16-20, 1994). 11pp. (ED 373 704)

Adults have specific and unique motivational needs in instructional settings. As a result, motivating instruction for adult learners should be designed with special considerations. This paper uses an adult motivational instructional design model to demonstrate the application of prescribed strategies into instructional software designed to teach basic statistics concepts. The ARCS (attention, relevance, confidence, and satisfaction) model for designing motivational strategies is described. For each category, an example is given for incorporating these motivational strategies into computer-based instruction programs. The implications and applications of motivating design of instruction for adults are also discussed.

Branch, R. C. et al. (1992). Instructional design practices and teacher planning routines, In: *Proceedings of Selected Research and Development Presentations at the Convention of the Association for Educational Communications and Technology and Sponsored by the Research and Theory Division.* Iowa. 10pp. (ED 347 976)

The hypothesis that the planning activities of classroom teachers correlate with the practices of instructional design professionals is explored within the context of this study. Classroom teachers participated in a survey which requested information regarding their planning routines. The 35-item two part questionnaire that was used as the data collection instrument was sent to 110 teachers currently teaching grades 7 through 12, including teachers participating in university-school partnership programs. The 61 who returned the questionnaires (56%) reported on their actions when planning to teach on a daily basis, and provided information on typical class size, number of years teaching, grade level, educational background, and subject taught. Analyses of the responses indicate that a strong correlation exists between teacher planning activities and instructional design practices, although the subject taught is the only variable studied that seems to affect the potential for teachers to practice instructional design. It is suggested that some instructional design practices may be beyond the realm of manipulation by public school teachers, and that a dialog between instructional design professionals should be formalized. It is also suggested that instructional designers should consider instructional design models that combine common teacher planning routines with instructional design practices.

Des Jardins, S., & Davis, H., Jr. (1995). Electronic performance support systems (EPSS): Making the transition. In: *Eyes on the Future: Converging Images, Ideas, and Instruction.* Selected Readings from the Annual Conference of the International Visual Literacy Association (27th, Chicago, IL, October 18-22, 1995). 9pp. (ED 391 499)

An electronic performance support system (EPSS) is a computerized system designed to increase productivity by supporting the performance of the worker on demand at the time of need. This way, workers are allowed to perform with a minimum of intervention from others. Popular examples of performance support tools, or partially implemented EPSSs, include the personal computer "wizards" whose assistance in creating a database, spreadsheet, document, or presentation results in a finished product rather than simply a user tutorial. An integrated performance support system, or a fully implemented EPSS, can provide even more: expert knowledge, searchable references and data, granular training like cue cards, and automated tools. A EPSS project begins with commitment to needs assessment and project support, cooperation between subject experts and designers, the skills of a multidisciplinary team, and a well-considered plan as to whether the system will be built from scratch or wrapped around an existing application. When marketing an EPSS, one must convince the organization that it will solve current performance problems, and that the level of support and the timing are optimal. Planning stages involve establishing project scope, reviewing organizational goals and needs, making sure the project team fully understands the reason for the EPSS, and creating mechanisms for reporting on progress. The next step is specification analysis, which involves feasibility studies, focus groups, task analysis, developing functional specifications, and choices of hardware and software. The results of the analyses are presented to the client, and if he or she decides to proceed with an EPSS, then the team can develop a maintenance strategy, prepare a development plan, and then actually build the system. Building includes developing the interface, the metaphor for the desktop, and data structure; it also comprises design and prototype, and procurement and integration of content into the system. Then the EPSS must be installed and systematically evaluated, with the team all the while alert to bio-factors in the work environment, like any dehumanizing effects of the system.

Earle, R. S. (1996). Instructional design fundamentals as elements of teacher planning routines: Perspectives and practices from two studies. In: *Proceedings of Selected Research and Development Presentations at the 1996 National Convention of the Association for Educational Communications and Technology* (18th, Indianapolis, IN, 1996). 11pp. (ED 397 789)

Teachers rely on mental planning throughout the design, implementation, and evaluation phases of instruction. This paper focuses on the elementary school teacher's use of instructional design (ID) skills in the planning and delivery of instruction, emphasizing the relative and "real" use of ID practices in both mental and written planning. Two studies of elementary school teachers, one involving 22 teachers from schools across North Carolina, the other involving 17 teachers from Provo School District in Utah, addressed planning issues and practices by yearly, unit, and daily planning. Results of both studies, illustrated in 12 data tables, indicated: (1) teachers favored mental planning; (2) plans were more specific at the unit and daily levels; (3) most teachers with formal training in ID felt it had improved their planning processes; (4) most teachers consciously used ID processes in planning; (5) the crucial elements of the ID process were goals, learner analysis, objectives, activities and strategies, tests, and revision; (6) ID processes received more attention at the unit and daily levels; (7) most teachers gave equal importance to written and mental planning; (8) during teaching there was less deviation from unit and daily plans than from yearly plans; (9) initial planning decisions centered around content and objectives, while most planning time was spent on content, materials, and activities; and (10) testing instruction prior to using it in the classroom was impractical. Ways for teachers and instructional designers to work together include: (1) developing a common technical language of instruction; (2) validating the scientific bases of teaching as essential precursors of the art of teaching; (3) adopting a layers-of-necessity philosophy in modifying classical ID to meet the needs and practices of teachers; and (4) recognizing the need for gradual reform and fundamental systemic restructuring as concurrent, interactive ventures.

Hong, E. (1992). Effects of Instructional Design with Mental Model Analysis on Learning. In: *Proceedings of Selected Research and Development Presentations at the Convention of the Association for Educational Communications and Technology and Sponsored by the Research and Theory Division*. Iowa. 25pp. (ED 347 994)

This paper presents a model for systematic instructional design that includes mental model analysis together with the procedures used in developing computer-based instructional materials in the area of statistical hypothesis testing. The instructional design model is based on the premise that the objective for learning is to achieve expert-like mental models, and instruction should be designed to help learners build relevant mental models in the specific domain. (The term mental model is defined as a person's internal, domain-specific representation that may be incomplete or unstable, and the term relevant mental model is defined as an internal, domain-specific representation that is relevant and useful for a person's subsequent understanding of and problem solving in the field.) It is proposed that mental model analysis be integrated into the design of instructional materials so that cognitive task analysis can be used to produce effective instructional strategies. The three phases in the design of instruction covered by the model are described: (1) analysis of instructional outcomes; (2) development of instructional material; and (3) implementation, evaluation, and revision of the instructional material. Seven procedures for applying this model are discussed in more detail: (1) identify instructional goals/objectives; (2) conduct mental model analysis; (3) identify the learners' entry level knowledge/skills; (4) develop instructional strategies considering mental models; (5) develop instructional materials and tests; (6) formative evaluation; and (7) revision of the instructional program. A discussion of the instructional effects which resulted from the application of the mental model strategies in an introductory statistics course concludes the paper.

Law, M. P. et al. (1995). Developing Electronic Performance Support Systems for Professionals. In: *Proceedings of the 1995 Annual National Convention of the Association for Educational Communications and Technology (AECT)*, (17th, Anaheim, CA, 1995). 8pp. (ED 383 317)

This paper discusses a variety of development strategies and issues involved in the development of electronic performance support systems (EPSS) for professionals. The topics of front-end analysis, development, and evaluation are explored in the context of a case study involving the development of an EPSS to support teachers in the use of alternative assessments. Strategies and concepts such as rapid prototyping, formative experimentation, usability, and socio-technical perspectives are highlighted. EPSS developers utilize principles found in instructional systems, software engineering, performance technology, and formative experimentation to develop an effective system for teachers. By making usability a goal and focusing on the social, organizational, and cultural factors that influence how work is performed by professionals in a specific work context, developers increase the likelihood of developing effective EPSSs that support the people and organization in meeting their goals. A figure illustrates the system prototype.

Moallem, M. (1996). Instructional design models and research on teacher thinking: Toward a new conceptual model for research and development. In: *Proceedings of Selected Research and Development Presentations at the 1996 National Convention of the Association for Educational Communications and Technology* (18th, Indianapolis, IN, 1996). 13pp. (ED 397 822)

Instructional designers believe that it is important to expose pre-service and in-service teachers to Instructional Systems Design (ISD) procedures and products so teachers can utilize them. Educational literature, however, reveals few attempts to relate instructional design theory and methods to teaching practice. This paper proposes a new conceptual model for thinking about teaching that incorporates current findings of research on teachers' thinking and components of instructional design models and principles. The paper reviews the major findings of research on teacher thinking and instructional systems design, and then presents a conceptual model to bring the two closely related fields together. Potential implications of the model for instructional development and research in instructional design and teacher thinking include: (1) teachers and their teaching and learning processes can only be studied within their social and cultural context; (2) teachers' knowledge is a complex blend of personal, practical, and theoretical knowledge—research in teaching, learning, and instruction has to shift its emphasis from cognition to social construction of knowing; (3) the image of teachers as designers of their own instruction needs to be emphasized in the instructional technology field, and the instructional design models and principles should be reconceptualized if they are to be used by teachers; (4) the concept of design as an artistic, social, and cooperative act should replace the procedural and technical concept of design—instructional design activities should focus on the product of the design instead of the procedure; and (5) instructional design models and principles should focus on an approach in which the design objectives and strategies or solutions evolve as the teacher-designer becomes more acquainted with the social and cultural system and subsystems, and people who are affected by the design, including learners, should participate in the decision-making process.

Rezabek, L. L., & Cochenour, J. J. (1996). Perceptions of the ID process: The influence of visual display. In: *Proceedings of Selected Research and Development Presentations at the 1996 National Convention of the Association for Educational Communications and Technology* (18th, Indianapolis, IN, 1996); see ED 397 772. 13pp. (ED 397 827)

This study was designed to investigate the influence of the visual display of an instructional design model on preservice teachers' perceptions of the instructional design process. Subjects were 36 undergraduate education majors enrolled in an introductory education class at a 4-year university. Students were first assessed on their initial knowledge and perceptions of the instructional design (ID) process. Students were then given a 3-hour introduction to ID. Afterwards, their perceptions were assessed again. Students viewed first one and then the second of two visual depictions of the Smith-Ragan ID model. One was drawn with curved lines and ovals and the other was formed with straight lines and rectangles. Half of the students were given the curve/oval model first, completed the assessment, and were then given the straight/rectangle model and asked the same questions. The other half of the students were presented with the models in reverse order. Results indicated that: preservice teachers changed their responses between the pretest and posttest assessing their perceptions of flexibility, organization, and value of the ID process; the straight/rectangle model was perceived to be more organized; and a majority of the students indicated a preference for the curve/oval model as the "best model to represent the ID process" and "choice of model to use to teach the ID process."

Richey, R. C. (1996). Robert M. Gagné's impact on instructional design theory and practice of the future. In: *Proceedings of Selected Research*

93

and Development Presentations at the 1996 National Convention of the Association for Educational Communications and Technology (18th, Indianapolis, IN, 1996). 12pp. (ED 397 828)

Robert Gagné has been a central figure in the infusion of instructional psychology into the field of instructional technology, and in the creation of the domain of instructional design. Gagné's design principles provide not only a theoretical orientation to an instructional design project, but also have prompted a number of design conventions and techniques. This paper examines the extent to which Gagné's theories continue to influence the field as design research expands and as design practice changes in response to new demands and pressures. Discussion includes the emerging tension between learner-oriented and content-oriented instruction trends in learner-centered instruction; the role of learner characteristics, learner involvement, and individualized instruction in Gagné's work; the emerging role of context in instructional design theory trends in context-centered instruction; the generic nature of Gagné's design theory and the de-emphasis of rooting design in a single context; the continuing dominance of Gagné's learning conditions, outcomes-based design, pre-design analysis, and Events of Instruction which provide a framework for creating those external conditions that promote learning; and the stability of Gagné's orientation to practice.

Scales, G. R. (1994).Trends in instructional technology: Educational reform and electronic performance support systems. In: *Proceedings of Selected Research and Development Presentations at the 1994 National Convention of the Association for Educational Communications and Technology Sponsored by the Research and Theory Division* (16th, Nashville, TN, February 16-20, 1994).12pp. (ED 373 756)

As society moves into the information age, changes need to be made in the educational process to ensure that students will have the skills they will need in the changing workplace. By keeping abreast of the changes in society, education, and training, instructional technology professionals can play a key role in restructuring the educational sys-

94

tem. This paper addresses two trends in the educational reform movement: integrating electronic technology in the classroom and the uses of electronic performance support systems (EPSS) as a tool for promoting training and support in education and in the workplace. An EPSS is an integrated electronic system that provides training and support at the moment of need for the employee. The concept of EPSS is examined, as well as its place in the educational process. Finally, the software development process and the need for change with the advent of such trends as EPSS are discussed.

Spector, J. M., et al. (1993). *An automated approach to instructional design guidance.* Paper presented at the Annual Meeting of the American Educational Research Association (Atlanta, GA, April 12-16, 1993).11pp. (ED 363 263)

This paper describes the Guided Approach to Instructional Design Advising (GAIDA), an automated instructional design tool that incorporates techniques of artificial intelligence. GAIDA was developed by the U.S. Air Force Armstrong Laboratory to facilitate the planning and production of interactive courseware and computer-based training materials. The tool is a case-based system that incorporates a short exposition of Gagné's nine events of instruction and four complete examples of applying the nine events to identification of naval insignia, classifications of electronic resistors, checklist procedure for the F-16 Gatling gun, and procedure for testing a patient's respiratory capacity using a spirometer. The paper covers (1) the issues involved in developing an automated instructional design advisor; (2) the results of Gagné's evaluation of the initial GAIDA case (the checklist for the F-16 gun); (3) a description of how GAIDA has been redesigned; and (4) how GAIDA will be used in future instructional design research and development projects.

Wilson, B.G. (1993). Constructivism and instructional design: Some personal reflections. In: *Proceedings of Selected Research and Development Presentations at the Convention of the Association for Educational Communications and Technology Sponsored by the Research and Theory*

Division (15th, New Orleans, Louisiana, January 13-17, 1993). 20pp. (ED 362 213)

Some personal reflections on instructional design and its relation to constructivism are explored. Instructional design in its present form is out of sync with the times in that its orientation, methods, and research base are behavioristic, or positivistic. However, a constructivist theory of instructional design is possible, particularly if constructivism is recognized as a philosophy rather than a strategy. To better fit the needs of practitioners, instructional design theories need to be better grounded in a broad understanding of learning and instructional processes. Generic principles and specific heuristics are needed for dealing with recurring problems and situations in instructional design practice. In addition, instructional design theories need to reflect instructional design as a profession. The theories of instructional design need to be adjusted or replaced with better ones that fit the newer understandings of learning and instruction.

ERIC Journal Articles

Barker, P., & Banerji, A. (1995). Designing electronic performance support systems. *Innovations in Education and Training International, 32*(1), 4-12. (EJ 501 748)

Outlines the basic nature of performance support and describes a generic model that can be used to facilitate electronic performance support system (EPSS) development. Performance measures are discussed; performance support guidelines are summarized; and a case study of the use of an EPSS is presented.

Chapman, B. L. (1995). Accelerating the design process: A tool for instructional designers. *Journal of Interactive Instruction Development, 8(2)*, 8-15. (EJ 520 294)

Discussion of instructional design for training focuses on the lack of tools that support the developmental phases of analysis, design, and evaluation. Topics include a standard instructional systems design model and an integrated software support system called "Designer's Edge," which focuses on the common activities of instructional designers.

Chiero, R. T. (1996). Electronic performance support systems: A new opportunity to enhance teacher effectiveness? *Action in Teacher Education, 17*(4), 37-44. (EJ 523 884)

Describes electronic performance support systems (EPSS) as an opportunity to view teacher preparation and support from a new perspective. EPSS are integrated, computer-based systems that provide timely information, useful advice, relevant instruction, and productivity tools when needed. Strengths and limitations of EPSS are discussed.

Ertmer, P. A., & Cennamo, K. S. (1995). Teaching instructional design: An apprenticeship model. *Performance Improvement Quarterly, 8*(4), 43-58. (EJ 512 311)

Discusses a cognitive apprenticeship approach to teaching design that incorporates elements of modeling, coaching, reflection, articulation, and exploration. Use of the model in an instructional design course that moves novice designers along a continuum of expertise is described, and it is suggested that the model could be adapted for performance technologists.

Holcomb, C. et al. (1996). ID activities and project success: Perceptions of practitioners. *Performance Improvement Quarterly, 9*(1), 49-61. (EJ 518 410)

Examines the relationship between instructional design (ID) activities and perceived project success. Results indicate that designers don't implement all the ID activities prescribed by traditional models and that certain activities are implemented more than others.

Lanzing, J. W. A., & Stanchev, I. (1994).Visual aspects of courseware engineering. *Journal of Computer Assisted Learning, 10* (2), 69-80. (EJ 486 731)

Discusses the possibilities for improving courseware and the courseware engineering process using visualization. Advantages and disadvantages of visualization are considered, including psychological, instructional, motivational, cross-cultural, and technical aspects; visual programming systems are described; adaptation and rapid prototyping are discussed; and directions for future research are suggested.

Price, R. V., & Repman, J. (1995). Instructional design for college-level courses using interactive television. *Journal of Educational Technology Systems, 23*(3), 251-63. (EJ 505 383)

Reviews instructional design models; discusses characteristics of distance education in higher education via interactive television; and presents a nine-step instructional design model designed specifically for college course delivery via interactive television. Course goals, content analysis, performance objectives, learner characteristics, lesson plans, and formative and summative evaluation are discussed.

Taylor, J. C. (1995). Distance education technologies: The fourth generation. *Australian Journal of Educational Technology, 11*(2), 1-7. (EJ 528 075)

Reviews developments in educational technology in distance education as an appropriate foundation for delineating the challenge to educators of conventional on-campus institutions interested in improving the quality of teaching and learning. Highlights include a conceptual framework of models of distance education, instructional design, and the need for organizational development.

Walster, D. (1995). Using instructional design theories in library and information science education. *Journal of Education for Library and Information Science, 36*(3), 239-48. (EJ 516 647)

Examines five instructional design theories and two emerging theoretical trends that are valuable to library and information science education. Describes the basic components of these theories and trends and discusses their applications in designing and implementing instruction in library and information science education and practice.

Witt, C. L., & Wager, W. (1994). A comparison of instructional systems design and electronic performance support systems design. *Educational Technology, 34*(6), 20-24. (EJ 488 241)

Compares the analysis, design, development, and evaluation of electronic performance support tools and systems to a traditional instructional systems design model. Topics discussed include indeterminate outcomes; rapid prototyping; front end analysis; intervention strategies; sequencing; user control; media selection; formative evaluation; and model validation.

How to Order ERIC Documents

Individual copies of ERIC documents are available in either microfiche or paper copy from the ERIC Document Reproduction Service (EDRS), 7420 Fullerton Road, Suite 110, Springfield, VA 22153-2852; some are available only in microfiche. Information needed for ordering includes the ED number, the number of pages, the number of copies wanted, the unit price, and the total unit cost. Sales tax should be included on orders from Maryland, Virginia, and Washington, DC.

Please order by ED number, indicate the format desired (microfiche or paper copy), and include payment for the price listed plus shipping. Call EDRS at 1-800-443-ERIC (or 703-440-1400) or e-mail EDRS customer service department: service@edrs.com, for information on pricing, shipping costs and/or other services offered by the contractor.

Inquiries about ERIC may be addressed to the ERIC Clearinghouse on

Information & Technology, 4-194 Center for Science and Technology, Syracuse University, Syracuse, NY 13244-4100 (800-464-9107), e-mail: eric@ericir.syr.edu; or ACCESS ERIC, 2277 Research Boulevard, 7A, Rockville, MD 20850 (800-LET-ERIC), e-mail: acceric@inet.ed.gov

What is ERIC?

ERIC, the Educational Resources Information Center, is a national education information system sponsored by the Office of Educational Research and Improvement in the U.S. Department of Education. The main product of ERIC is a bibliographic database containing citations and abstracts for over 950,000 documents and journal articles published since 1966. Most of the document literature cited in ERIC can be read in full text at any of the 900+ libraries or institutions worldwide holding the ERIC microfiche collection. In addition, users can purchase copies of ERIC documents from the ERIC Document Reproduction Service. Journal articles cited in ERIC can be obtained at a subscribing library, through interlibrary loan, or from an article reprint service

How do I find information in ERIC?

The ERIC Database can be searched manually through its two print indexes, *Resources in Education* (RIE) and *Current Index to Journals in Education* (CIJE). Over 3,000 libraries and information centers subscribe to one or both of these monthly indexes. The database can also be searched online: (a) through a computer based information retrieval service; (b) by CD-ROM; (c) on a locally mounted system, which may be accessible through the Internet; or (d) Internet: http://ericir.syr.edu/Eric/. The number of libraries offering online and CD-ROM search services is rapidly increasing.

What is ERIC/IT?

The ERIC Clearinghouse on Information & Technology, or ERIC/IT, is one of 16 clearinghouses in the ERIC system. It specializes in library and information science and educational technology. ERIC/IT acquires, selects, catalogs, indexes, and abstracts documents and journal articles in these subject areas for input into the ERIC database.

Among the topics covered in **library and information science** are:

• management, operation, and use of libraries and information centers

• library technology and automation

• library education

• information policy

• information literacy

• information storage, processing and retrieval

• networking

Topics covered in **educational technology** include:

• design, development, and evaluation of instruction

• computer-assisted instruction

• hypermedia, interactive video, and interactive multimedia

• telecommunications

• film, radio, television, and other audio-visual media

101

- distance education

- simulation and gaming

What is available from ERIC/IT?

Each year, ERIC/IT publishes Monographs, Minibibliographies Digests, and in the fields of educational technology and library and information science. Our semiannual newsletter, ERIC/IT Update, announces new clearinghouse products and developments, and ERIC/IT Networkers provide helpful information for using ERIC-related resources on the Internet.

Publications

- Digests, providing brief overviews of topics of current interest and references for further reading

- Monographs, featuring trends and issues analyses, synthesis papers and annotated bibliographies

- ERIC/IT Update, a semi-annual newsletter

User Services

- Response to inquiries about ERIC and matters within the ERIC/IT scope area

- Workshops and presentations about ERIC and database searching

- Assistance in searching the ERIC database

AskERIC

• Internet-based question answering service for educators

• AskERIC Virtual Library, an Internet site of education-related information resources including lesson plans, InfoGuides, listservs and much more

E-mail: askeric@askeric.org

Internet: http://www.askeric.org

Would you like to submit your work to ERIC?

Have you written materials related to educational technology or library and information science that you would like to share with others? ERIC/IT would be interested in reviewing your work for possible inclusion in the ERIC database. We actively solicit documents from researchers, practitioners, associations, and agencies at national, state, and local levels. ERIC documents include the following and more:

• Research Reports

• Program Descriptions

• Instructional Materials

• Conference Papers

• Teaching Guides

• Opinion Papers

How do I find out more?

For additional information about ERIC or about submitting documents, or for a current publications list, contact:

ERIC Clearinghouse on Information & Technology

Syracuse University

4-194 Center for Science and Technology

Syracuse, New York 13244-4100

Michael B. Eisenberg, Director

Telephone: (315) 443-3640   Fax: (315) 443-5448

             (800) 464-9107

Internet: eric@ericir.syr.edu

             http://ericir.syr.edu/ithome

Questions about the ERIC system can also be directed to:

ACCESS ERIC

2277 Research Boulevard, 7A

Rockville, Maryland 20850

Telephone: (800) LET-ERIC

Internet: acceric@inet.ed.gov

             http://www.aspensys.com/eric/

ERIC Clearinghouses

- Adult, Career, and Vocational Education

- Assessment and Evaluation

- Community Colleges

- Counseling and Student Services

- Disabilities and Gifted Education

- Educational Management

- Elementary and Early Childhood Education

- Higher Education

- Information & Technology

- Languages and Linguistics

- Reading, English, and Communication

- Rural Education and Small Schools

- Science, Mathematics, and Environmental Education

- Social Studies/Social Science Education

- Teaching and Teacher Education

- Urban Education

Support Components

• ERIC Document Reproduction Service

   Telephone: (800) 443-ERIC (3742)

• ERIC Processing and Reference Facility

   Telephone: (800) 799-ERIC (3742)